D1391498

THE CONCISE
DAY SKIPPER
GUIDE

The Author

Mike Bowyer first went to sea as an apprentice in the Merchant Navy in 1947, gained his Master's Foreign Going Certificate and was a Navigating Officer with the Union Castle Mail Steamship Company until 1962, when he left the sea to pursue a new career in teaching. Now Deputy Head of a Special School in the South of England, one of his many duties is introducing the young people to the experience of sailing. As an Instructor for the RYA/DTI Shore Based Yachtmaster courses (both Offshore and Ocean) for over twenty years he has also introduced many adults to the practical side of sailing. Mike keeps an Achilles 24 in Cornwall, which he sails with his wife and young son. He has cruised extensively in the English and Scottish waters and the Mediterranean. He is also Chairman of the Berkshire branch of the Sail Training Association.

The Concise Day Skipper Guide

A study and revision aid for the RYA Day Skipper and Watch Leader shore based course

by Mike Bowyer

DAVID & CHARLES

Newton Abbot London North Pomfret (Vt)

Photoset and printed in Great Britain
by Redwood Burn Limited, Trowbridge, Wiltshire
for David & Charles Publishers plc
Brunel House, Newton Abbot, Devon

British Library Cataloguing in Publication Data

Bowyer, Mike
Concise day skipper guide.
1. Seamanship: For yachting
I. Title
623.88′223

ISBN 0 7153 9055 4

Published in the United States of America
by David & Charles Inc
North Pomfret   Vermont 05053   USA

Contents

The Course

This book is intended to help anyone following the RYA Day Skipper/Watch Leader Shore Based Course in order to obtain a course completion certificate.

The course, together with the complementary practical course, sets a minimum standard of competence for those intending to take charge of a small boat at sea during daylight hours (Day Skippers). In the case of those going to sea in larger vessels it measures the ability to take charge of a watch. However, both the Day Skipper shore based and practical courses are best regarded as a preliminary stage towards the more advanced qualification of Coastal Skipper and Yachtmaster Offshore.

The information is presented as concisely as possible as an aid to self-study and revision and it follows the syllabus through in the same order as it is set out in the RYA Log Book which all students should have to record their progress. The aim has been to provide the essential basic information required to complete the course successfully without frills or digressions. It follows that many students will want to read up more fully on some subjects in some of the many excellent yachting publications available. In particular all students will be advised, in connection with this book, to make themselves familiar with one of the commonly used nautical almanacs, such as Reed's, and become aware of the information in them and its lay-out.

Practical Experience

Neither this book nor the shore based course itself can replace the practical experience which is necessary, but only be a preparation for it. Five day practical courses leading to formal qualification are offered by many clubs and sailing schools. It is also necessary to take every opportunity of sailing with an experienced skipper and getting as much practice in boat-handling as possible. Before you can take the practical course you must have logged at least 15 days sea time,

including 200 miles of sailing and 8 hours of night sailing. Complete your log book each time you go to sea and get it signed by the skipper to show you have done this.

Questions and Exercises

At the end of each chapter are questions or navigation exercises with answers at the end of the book. All the navigation exercises are on Admiralty Practice Chart No. 5052 (Dover Strait).

A section of this chart is shown on pages 58 and 59 for reference while studying the text but readers should purchase a copy of the chart to complete the exercises. The chart is Crown copyright and reproduced with permission of the Controller of Her Majesty's Stationery Office.

Tidal information is reproduced from
Reed's Nautical Almanac by kind
permission of the publishers.

1
NAUTICAL TERMS

Common nautical terms familiar to all seafarers need to be understood so that when orders are given or messages relayed everybody knows precisely what is meant.

Parts of a boat

Study the keyed diagram below and learn the names of various parts of the hull and sails. Then make yourself familiar with the following terminology.

Directional words

Aft: – towards the stern of the boat.
Abeam – at right angles to the fore and aft line of the boat.
Aloft – up the mast or in the rigging.
Ahead – directly in front of your boat.
Astern – directly behind your boat.
Abeam – to the side, more or less at right angles to the fore and aft line of the vessel.
Forward – towards the bow of the vessel (pronounced 'forrard')
Port – the left hand side of the vessel looking forward.
Starboard – the right hand side of the vessel looking forward.
On the port (or starboard) bow – ahead of your boat at an angle to the bows, but forward of the beam.
On the port (or starboard) quarter – at an angle to the stern of your boat, but abaft the beam.
Windward – the direction from which the wind is coming.
Leeward – the opposite direction to windward.

11

Parts of a Boat, Hull, Rig and Sails

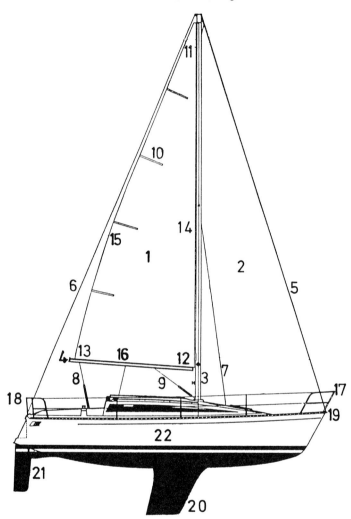

1. Mainsail	9. Kicking Strap	17. Pulpit
2. Foresail (Jib, Genoa)	10. Batten	18. Pushpit
3. Mast	11. Head	19. Rubbing Piece
4. Boom	12. Tack	20. Keel
5. Forestay	13. Clew	21. Rudder
6. Backstay	14. Luff	22. Hull
7. Shrouds	15. Leach	
8. Main Sheet	16. Foot	

Sailing Terms

Beating – sailing towards the wind with the sails hauled in tight.

Broaching – when running before a strong wind to be suddenly brought broadside on.

Broad Reach – sailing with the wind on the quarter.

Close hauled – sailing as near into the wind as possible without the sails flapping. A boat may be said to be on the port tack or the starboard tack according to which side the wind is blowing from.

Tacking – the process by which a sailing vessel can go to windward, making a series of zig-zag 'tacks' or 'boards' at an angle to the wind.

Starboard tack – sailing with the wind on the starboard side and the sails set on the port side.

Port tack – sailing with the wind on the port side and the sails set on the starboard side.

Go About – to change tack by altering course to bring the wind on the other side of the bow.

Running – to sail with the wind dead astern.

Gybe – to alter course when sailing with the wind abaft the beam by steering to put the stern through the wind and transferring the boom to the other side. A gybe can be accidental when sailing with the wind dead aft.

To luff – to steer close up into the wind. Often done to relieve wind pressure on the sails while they are adjusted.

Bear away – to alter course away from the wind.

Pay off – let the sails fill and sail away on a new tack.

In stays – when the bows point directly into the wind with the sails flapping during the process of going about.

In irons – when the boat is caught in stays and refuses to pay off on either tack.

Goose winging – to set the mainsail on one side of the boat and the foresail the other when running.

Give way – to alter course in order to concede right of way to another vessel.

Stand on – to maintain the course and speed of your vessel because you have right of way.

Under way – commonly describes any vessel moving through the water. Strictly speaking it refers to any vessel not actually anchored or tied up.

Heave to – to stop or slow the vessel by coming head to wind, and laying with the headsail aback and the tiller to leeward. Sometimes done to ride out heavy weather, but can be for any reason such as waiting for a tide or simply taking things easy while you have tea.

Aback – said of a sail which is deliberately set with the wind on the wrong side or is accidentally 'taken aback' by a shift of wind or movement of the helm.

Mooring terms

Anchor buoy – a small buoy attached by a light line to the anchor which enables you to see where your anchor is lying.

Anchor aweigh – the anchor is said to be aweigh at the point when it breaks out of the sea bed when it is being hauled in.

Breast line – mooring ropes which lie at right angles from the vessel to the jetty.

Backspring – mooring rope which leads either from the after part of the boat to a point on the jetty forward of the boat, or vice versa.

Make fast – to secure the boat with mooring lines to the jetty or to tie up to a buoy.

Let go – an order to drop the anchor, or an order to slip the mooring lines or let loose from a buoy in order to proceed.

Ropework

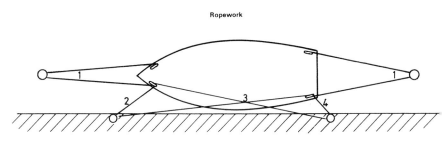

1. Ropes to Piles   2. Bowline   3. Backsprings   4. Sternline

+ 2 Spare lines

Points of Sailing

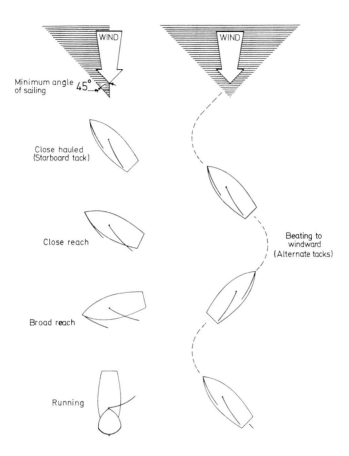

Questions

1 The skipper tells you to luff-up. What should you do?
2 Name three points of sailing
3 Name some of the lines used in mooring a vessel
4 You are sailing on the port tack. On which side of the boat is the boom?
5 What would you be doing if you were goosewinging?

2
ROPEWORK

Candidates are expected to understand the properties of synthetic ropes, to be able to tie and know the correct use of the more common knots and be proficient at general rope handling.

Properties of ropes

Natural fibre ropes such as manilla and hemp have almost entirely disappeared and all those used by the modern yachtsman are likely to be synthetic. These are stronger and less subject to rot. Many of them are 'hawser laid' in the traditional rope making way, that is twisted in three strands. Other modern man-made fibre ropes are plaited and others have a more complex braided construction. Synthetic ropes are so strong that a close calculation of breaking strains is no longer the worry it was for small boat skippers. Nevertheless an adequate rope for the job must be chosen. One of the other main differences between them which influences choice for a particular job is the degree to which they will stretch. The main types to be acquainted with are:

Nylon Will also be encountered under brand names like polyamide, bri-nylon, enkalon, etc. Very strong and hard wearing. Has a great deal of stretch which makes it suitable for anchoring, mooring and towing. The hawser laid nylon ropes tend to be stiff to handle when wet but the plaited and braided varieties are more flexible.

Polyester Will also be found under brands names like dacron and terylene. Not quite as strong as nylon, but probably the best all purpose rope for small cruising yachts. Handles easily and resists wear well. It has a low stretch characteristic making it suitable for halliards and sheets.

Polypropylene Will also be found under branded names like novolen and polital. Not so strong as the other two, but cheaper and is a useful rope for some tasks like dinghy painters and lashings. A special characteristic is that it floats which makes it suitable for some special jobs like lines for lifebelts.

Rope Requirements

Mooring Lines An adequate supply of mooring lines for the average small cruising yacht would comprise 2 short ropes as bow and stern line (say 4 metres), 2 long ropes for backsprings (length of your boat plus another 3 or 4 metres). These may also be needed for mooring between piles.

2 spare lines 8 or 10 metres each. When not in use mooring lines should be carefully coiled in the cockpit or in after locker. Recommended types would be three strand polyester multi-plait nylon. 12mm diameter would be adequate for a 7 metre yacht, 14mm for one of 10 metres.

Mooring Lines Diagram

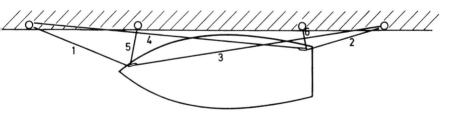

1. Bowline
2. Sternline
3. Forward Backspring
4. After Backspring
5. Forward Breastrope
6. Aft Breastrope

Halliards Each sail has its own halliard by which it is hoisted and lowered. It is essential they run smoothly through the blocks and they must be coiled carefully to make sure they do not snarl up when needed. A braided polyester like Marlowbraid or a pre-stretched 3 strand polyester is most suitable. A 7 or 8 metre yacht should have 8mm halliards and a 10 metre yacht 10mm halliards. Alternative spelling 'halyards'.

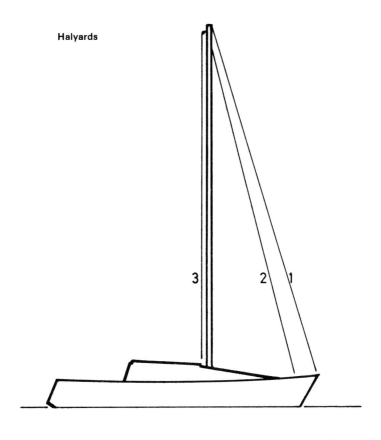

Halyards

1. Jib Halyard   2. Spinnaker Halyard   3. Main Halyard

Sheets Sheets are the ropes which control the sails, hauling them in or slackening off as the wind or the sailing direction changes. These are the ropes most frequently used and need to be kind to the hands. Braided or plaited polyester is best. The mainsheet usually runs through two or more blocks to give a mechanical advantage when hauling. For all yachts up to 10 metres a size of 10mm would be adequate. Headsails have two sheets leading aft down each side of deck, the leeward one being hauled in with each change of tack. On most yachts they tail back to a winch so they can be set up tight. Standard jib sheets should be the same size as the mainsheet. Genoas (a big form of jib) and spinnakers (special headsails for running down wind) should have sheets one size thicker. Sheets must always be coiled tidily so they are free to run.

Sheets

1. Main Sheet　　**2. Jib Sheets**　　**3. Spinnaker Sheets**

Anchor Warps See next chapter for relative merits of chain and rope. If rope is used a multiplait or three strand nylon is best. For a 7 metre yacht 12mm diameter will be needed and for a 10 metre boat 16mm. For a day cruiser the minimum amount that should be carried is enough to anchor in 10 metres depth, or about 50 metres. The inboard end of the warp (called the **bitter end**) must be securely fastened inboard, preferably with a stout lashing which can be cut free to abandon the anchor in emergency.

Care of Ropes

The biggest enemy of rope is chafe which can damage and weaken it very quickly. Regular inspection of all ropes which come under tension is advisable. Mooring lines, anchor warps and other ropes passing through fairleads are especially vulnerable and can be given protection at the point of chafe by wrapping a piece of sacking or sailcloth round them. Mooring lines in permanent use in the home berth can be protected by fitting a piece of plastic hose over them at vulnerable places.

Sheets and halliards are subject to wear where they pass through blocks. It is a good idea to end for end them once or twice during the season. Ropes will also suffer in the long term from internal chafe caused by sand, dirt and salt residues. To prolong life wash them down well with fresh water at the end of each season and hang them up to dry properly.

Knots

Figure of Eight Knot. Mainly used as a stopper knot on the ends of sheets to prevent them running out through the block. Does not jam and can be easily untied.

Reef knot. Used for joining two ropes of equal thickness. Typical example is for tying reef points from which it takes its name. Will not slip however hard you pull, and will not jam so is easy to undo.

Clove Hitch. It has many uses including securing fenders to a guard rail, securing a dinghy painter to a post, rigging lifelines between stanchions, lashing the tiller, etc. It is a knot always tied round a standing object. It is not safe to tie with a short end as motion may cause it to jerk undone. It can be difficult to untie if it has been under heavy strain.

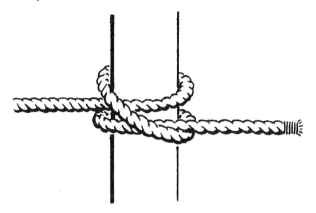

Rolling Hitch. Similar to a clove hitch but with an extra turn. Used whenever you need to attach a rope to another of the same or larger diameter, securing a rope back on itself or for tying round a spar or other object when the strain is going to come parallel with it.

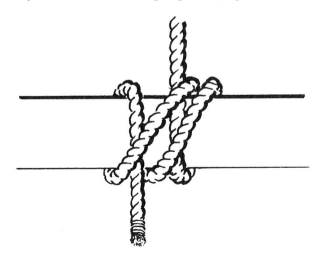

Single and Double Sheet Bends. A single sheet bend is used for joining two ropes together, either of equal or different thickness. If they are different thicknesses the thicker one should form the bight. It can also be formed through an eye to fasten sheets to sails. A double sheet bend gives extra security and is often used for connecting a rope to a bosun's chair. If these knots are used to join ropes made of different materials it is advisable to seize the ends by lashing them to the standing part with twine.

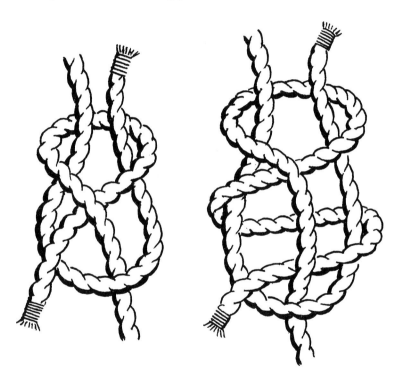

Bowline. To be used whenever you want a loop in a rope that will not slip. Common uses are to slip mooring lines over bollards and making jib sheets fast to the clew of the sail. Can also be tied round the body as a personal life line. It is a knot which you should learn to do thoroughly with your eyes closed so you can tie it without hesitation in any situation.

Round Turn and Two Half Hitches. For tying a rope to a ring or spar. It is commonly used to make fast a dinghy painter to a mooring buoy or to a ring on a quay. It will never come undone and will untie easily even under tension.

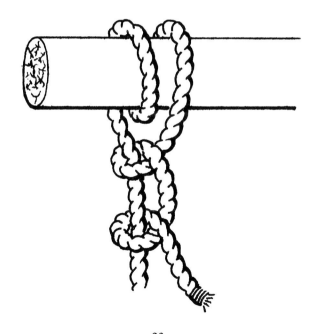

Rope Handling

Coiling. It is essential to safety and good seamanship that all ropes on a yacht are ready for immediate use and will not become tangled at a critical moment. Always form coils in laid (three strand) ropes in a clockwise direction. It will lay naturally that way. Take the end in one hand and form a loop of convenient size, then gathering up two or three feet of rope at a time, depending on the size of the coil, place them on your hand next to the original coil, making sure each coil is roughly the same size.

Thick ropes are best coiled down on the deck. Braided and plaited ropes do not need to be coiled clockwise and in fact are best done in alternate directions to avoid an inclination to kink. Coiling ropes which are fast at one end, like sheets and halliards, must always be done starting at the standing end.

Sheet coils are usually placed on deck. Make sure they are put down the right way up for the sheet to run out from the top. Halliard coils are usually hung from the halliard cleat. To do this you reach through the coil and take hold of a loop of the standing end, pull this through the coil and pass it over the top to fasten it on the top peg of the cleat, twisting it as you do so to form a half hitch. This neatly hangs the coil from the cleat and all you have to do to clear the halliard for use is to throw off this loop.

Coils of rope which are not needed for immediate use can have a half hitch made round them with their own end. Large coils to be stowed in lockers are best dealt with by making a seizing of twine at two or three places round the coil, otherwise they soon become tangled when stowed with other gear. One emergency coil should however always be ready for immediate use.

Untidy heaps of rope may trip up crew on deck and even cause them to fall overboard and may cause an emergency if they snarl up in the middle of a critical operation. Before setting off or starting your engine always check that no ropes are trailing in the water to foul the propeller. If you are towing a dinghy make sure the painter is not trailing.

Throwing A Rope. Situations arise where it is necessary to pass a line to the shore or to another vessel. This could be when you are giving or accepting a tow, or getting a line to someone on a jetty who will make you fast alongside. The only reliable way of doing this is as follows. Make sure you have a neatly coiled rope which will run freely. Slit the coil in two and take one half in your left hand and the other in your right. Gain some momentum with a swinging motion of your right arm and then let go the right hand coil with a forward fling. As it flakes out ahead let the left hand coil go to follow it.

Cleating. A common mistake when making fast ropes on cleats is to put on too many turns, thinking that this makes it more secure. It will not in fact do so and too many turns will hinder work if you want to use the rope quickly. The correct way to make up a rope on a cleat is to take one turn straight round the cleat and then two figure of eight turns, finishing off with a turn of the rope in the form of a half hitch over one arm of the cleat, so that the end of the rope passes under the standing part. This last action is the locking or jamming turn and guards against the coils working loose and coming off the cleat. Some experienced seamen regard the locking hitch as controversial in case it is troublesome to undo in emergency, but it makes for neater stowage and there should be no harm in using it in most circumstances.

Winches. Winches are used on most yachts these days for main halliards and jib sheets. Because their purpose is to achieve tightness in the luff of the mainsail or the setting of the jib it follows that there is a good deal of tension involved and they must be used properly.

Sheet winches usually rotate clockwise so one turn of the sheet must be taken round the drum in that direction. When it is hauled just tight by hand two or three more turns should be put on and the winch handle inserted. Then one person should maintain the tension by tailing on the running end and gathering in more rope as the other winches away. It is possible for one person to winch and tail, but much easier with two. When the sail is tight enough the running end is cleated and the winch handle removed.

When the time comes to ease or slack off the sheet, remember the tension you have put on it by winching. It must be eased out, not just cast off. As you take off the turn on the cleat hold on to the sheet between the drum and the cleat to keep the tension. Then gently ease away with the turns still on the drum until you feel that all the tension has gone, when you can then safely cast them off.

Halliard winches are controlled in the same manner. The halliard can usually be hoisted by hand most of the way, the winch just being used for the final tension of the luff. When lowering the sail the same precautions apply. Keep control of the halliard by holding it between the cleat and the drum and ease it away gently.

This principle should be applied to handling ropes with weight on them in all circumstances, whether there is a winch or not. If you are lowering or hoisting a heavy weight, or handling a boat being towed, never rely on your own strength or the rope will probably be snatched out of your hand. Always take a turn round something like a cleat or handy spar. Then you can hoist away in safety while somebody tails on the rope and gathers in the turns you have gained. When lowering or easing off, the turns act as a friction brake which you can easily control. This is known as **surging**.

Questions

1 What are the halliards used for?
2 What are sheets?
3 What is the best rope for an anchor warp?
4 What would you use a bowline for?
5 What knot would you tie at the end of the sheets?

3
ANCHOR WORK

The syllabus calls for a knowledge of different types of anchor and the considerations that have to be taken into account when anchoring.

The main anchor of a vessel is known as the **bower**. All well equipped small boats will carry a second which is known as the **kedge**. The latter is usually lighter as it may have to be rowed out and dropped from the dinghy. The kedge can be used as a second anchor in severe conditions or poor holding ground. Or it can be **streamed** (laid out) with the bower in a way which will restrict swinging in a narrow channel or used as a stern anchor if the yacht is moored with headlines to a quay as is necessary in some crowded ports. The other use of the kedge is to haul off a yacht which is aground by dropping it in deep water with the dinghy and then hauling up to it. The same technique can be used to manoeuvre a sailing boat out of a restricted anchorage if no engine is available.

Types of Anchor

Fisherman's. This is the traditional type of anchor and not now much used by yachtsmen. To stow flat on deck it has to have the stock unshipped and this then has to be put back in place and secured before the anchor can be used. You also need quite a heavy one to be efficient. Consequently the more modern stockless types of anchor are now preferred. Regarded by many as still the best anchor for a rocky bottom, but not so efficient as others in sand and mud. A yacht of 5 to 8 metres would need a fisherman's anchor of 25kg.

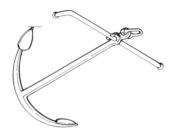

CQR. The most popular and longest established stockless anchor for small craft invented in the 1950s. Distinctively shaped like a ploughshare and is known in some countries as a **plough** anchor. Will hold well on most bottoms except rock. 15g would be sufficient size for a 5 to 8 metre yacht.

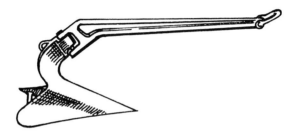

Danforth. The advantage of this anchor is that it folds flat and is easy to stow. The design also makes it less likely to be fouled by its own cable than most other anchors. Its holding characteristics are similar to those of the CQR though some consider it has rather less efficiency weight for weight.

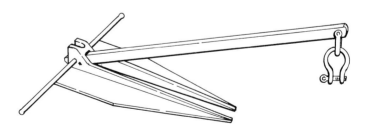

Meon. Similar in design and performance to the Danforth, but with several shorter flukes instead of two long ones.

28

Bruce. A relatively new invention which has gained a good reputation. In shape it is rather like a huge claw and it scores in having a better power/weight ratio than the others. It will hold fairly well on rock and very well on most other bottoms. A 10kg size would be adequate for a 5 to 8 metre yacht.

Anchor Cables

Chain is held to be preferable as an anchor cable, but impracticable to stow in small yachts. Its efficiency is not so much to do with its strength as its weight, which results in a better **catenary** or curve in the cable underwater, imparting a straight pull on the anchor which digs it further in rather than pulling it out. You can usually anchor by paying out three times the depth of water with chain, but five times the depth is recommended for a rope warp. The performance of rope can be greatly improved by having a short length of chain at the anchor end.

Anchor cables should be code-marked at every two metres so you know how much you are paying out. Chain can be painted – paint two links at two metres, four links at four metres and so forth. With rope this can be done by sewing in lengths of twine, or perhaps scraps of different coloured material for each mark.

When coming up to an anchorage have the anchor cable flaked out on the foredeck, checking that the anchor is properly made fast and the cable clear to run. A member of the crew should be standing by to drop the anchor and understand that they must not do so until given the word by the skipper.

Anchor Buoys

It often pays to know just where your anchor is on the sea bottom. This can be done by attaching an anchor marker by a line (the length of the maximum depth of water) to the ring in the crown of the anchor. At the other end attach a small buoy. One can be improvised with a plastic container or dinghy fender. The buoy will float directly above the anchor or nearly so and marking the position in this way can be useful to a skipper leaving a crowded or confined anchorage. The buoy will tell him where the yacht will be when the cable is hauled in and the anchor breaks out of the ground.

Anchor buoys can also be a boon if the anchor should become foul of rocks or mooring tackle, etc on the sea bed and cannot be hauled up by the cable. In these circumstances going out in the dinghy and pulling on the anchor buoy line will often be sufficient to 'trip' the anchor and pull it clear. In fact the arrangement is often referred to as a tripping line. It may not be wise to use them in harbours with lots of motor boat traffic as there is a risk of the line fouling somebody's propeller.

Where to anchor

Considerations to be borne in mind in deciding on an anchorage.

Shelter If the wind is strong you will want to be sheltered from it and also away from any strong tidal flow. Study the weather forecast and check what future wind direction and strength may be during your stay. Never anchor on an exposed lee shore in a strong wind and make sure that a change of conditions does not leave you in that situation.

Nature of bottom What is the sea bed composed of? The chart will tell you with abbreviations – s. for sand, sh. for shingle and so on. Sand and mud offer the best holding ground. Avoid if possible anchoring on a rocky bottom as the anchor may foul and be difficult to get up. Charts are sometimes marked with a small anchor showing a recommended spot. Pilot books also give guidance.

Depth of water When the tide falls will there be enough water to keep you afloat? Even if your yacht will take the ground upright you may not want to wait until high water before you can sail again. How to make the right calculations will be found in the chapter on tides. Think also about the depth of water around you. As the yacht swings and lays back on her warp with the effect of wind and tide she may be in shallower water.

Swinging room. If other vessels are anchored or moored to buoys you will have to choose a spot where there is room for you to swing right round your anchor in a circle when you are laying well back on your anchor cable. You will swing constantly with variations of wind and tide. Of course all the others will swing as well, but owing to differences of design they will not all swing at the same time or in the same direction. Anchored boats can swing very fast and do considerable damage in colliding with another, so it is important to leave plenty of room. It is equally important to ensure you will swing clear of any other objects like navigation marks, the ends of jetties, etc.

Foul ground. These words sometimes appear on the chart and indicate that the bottom is littered with some debris or obstruction which makes anchoring undesirable for fear of the anchor becoming fast. It is also unwise to anchor anywhere you see from the chart or sign on the shore that there is an underwater cable or pipeline.

Other traffic. It is inconsiderate to anchor in a busy fairway or narrow channel and might be a breach of regulations (see chapter on International Regulations). Vessels should indicate to others that they are anchored by showing a black ball during daylight and at night an all round white light.

How to Anchor

Having chosen the place you want to anchor work out the depth of cable you will need initially and flake it out. It pays to sail round the anchorage a couple of times taking in all the conditions and choosing the best spot. Drop the anchor while there is still a little way on the vessel so that it bites into the ground, then wait for the chain or warp to tighten as she drops back. If there is not a lot of wind or tide you can use the engine to go very gently astern for a few revs in order to lay out the cable and ensure it is not in a heap on bottom. Before you can relax you must make sure the anchor is holding and not dragging. You can do this by taking a bearing of a fixed object on the shore. This should remain fairly constant. An alternative is by transit, that is lining up two objects ashore and making sure they stay in line. Check again after a change of tide.

It is wise also to find the depth of water by echo sounder or lead line and confirm your tidal calculations to be sure you will be afloat at low water and have enough cable out for high water.

31

If you go ashore when anchored off a beach remember that sea conditions can change very quickly and make it tricky getting back aboard from a dinghy. It is a wise precaution to leave one member of the crew on board to make sure the vessel is safe and to pay out more cable if she starts to drag.

Questions

1 What precautions must you take when anchoring?
2 What are the best holding grounds for an anchor?
3 What is an anchor buoy used for?
4 What lights should you show at night if you were in a small boat at anchor?
5 How can you measure how much anchor chain or rope is let go?

LATERAL BUOYAGE

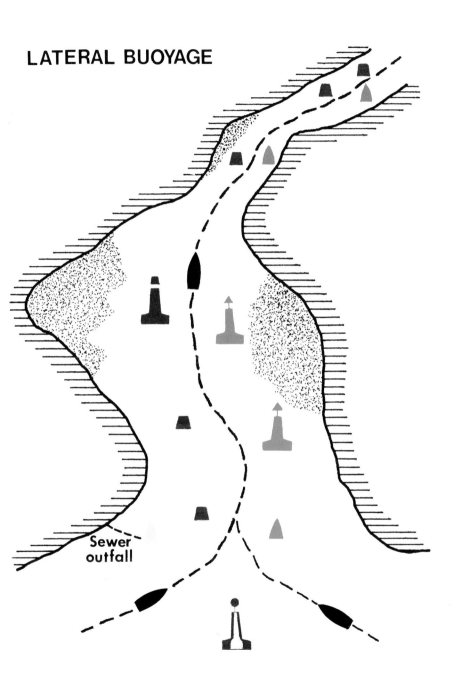

Sewer
outfall

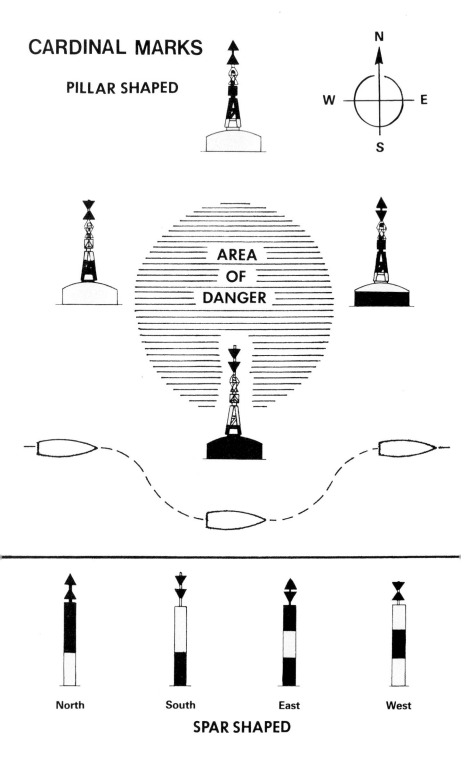

CARDINAL MARKS

PILLAR SHAPED

N

W   E

S

AREA
OF
DANGER

North   **South**   **East**   **West**

SPAR SHAPED

International Code Flags and Meanings

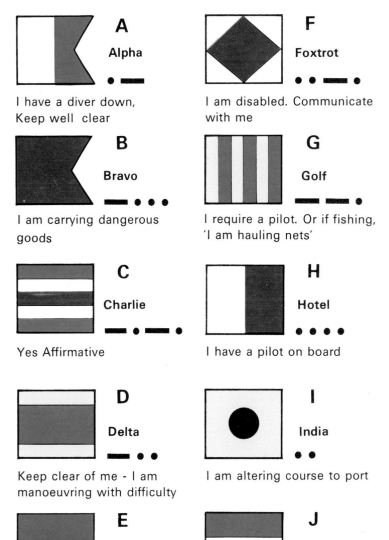

A Alpha

I have a diver down, Keep well clear

B Bravo

I am carrying dangerous goods

C Charlie

Yes Affirmative

D Delta

Keep clear of me - I am manoeuvring with difficulty

E Echo

I am altering course to starboard

F Foxtrot

I am disabled. Communicate with me

G Golf

I require a pilot. Or if fishing, 'I am hauling nets'

H Hotel

I have a pilot on board

I India

I am altering course to port

J Juliett

I am on fire and have a dangerous cargo on board, keep clear of me

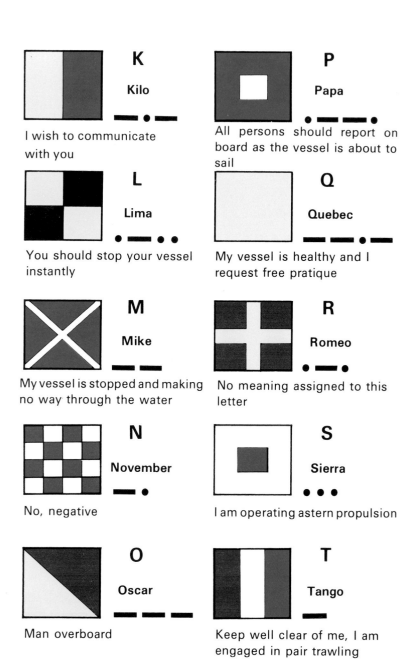

K Kilo

I wish to communicate with you

L Lima

You should stop your vessel instantly

M Mike

My vessel is stopped and making no way through the water

N November

No, negative

O Oscar

Man overboard

P Papa

All persons should report on board as the vessel is about to sail

Q Quebec

My vessel is healthy and I request free pratique

R Romeo

No meaning assigned to this letter

S Sierra

I am operating astern propulsion

T Tango

Keep well clear of me, I am engaged in pair trawling

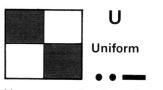

U
Uniform

● ● ▬

You are running into danger

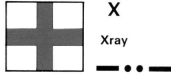

X
Xray

▬ ● ● ▬

Stop carrying out your intentions and watch for my signals

V
Victor

● ● ● ▬

I require assistance

Y
Yankee

▬ ● ▬ ▬

I am dragging my anchor

W
Whisky

● ▬ ▬

I require medical assistance

Z
Zulu

▬ ▬ ▬ ● ●

I require a tug. When made by fishing vessels 'I am shooting nets'

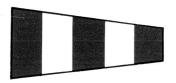

Code and answering pendant

Note. Not all the single letter signals may be made by Morse as an alternative to the flags. Letters B, C, D, E, G, H, I, M, S, T & Z have meanings in the Collision Regulations and should only be made by sound in that context.

VESSEL	LIGHTS/ASPECT				SOUND SIGNAL IN FOG	SHAPE (IF ANY)
	AHEAD	ASTERN	PORT	ST'B'D		
POWER DRIVEN						
POWER DRIVEN (less than 12m)					an efficient sound signal	
POWER DRIVEN TOWING				200m+		200m+
BEING TOWED						200m+
SAILING						

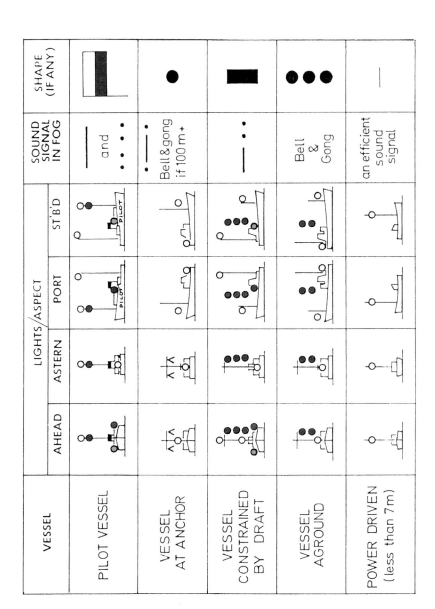

| VESSEL | LIGHTS/ASPECT | | | | SOUND SIGNAL IN FOG | SHAPE (IF ANY) |
	AHEAD	ASTERN	PORT	ST'B'D		
PILOT VESSEL					___ and • • • •	
VESSEL AT ANCHOR					• • • Bell & gong if 100 m+	●
VESSEL CONSTRAINED BY DRAFT					• • ___	■
VESSEL AGROUND					Bell & Gong	● ● ●
POWER DRIVEN (less than 7m)					an efficient sound signal	___

VESSEL	LIGHTS/ASPECT				SOUND SIGNAL IN FOG	SHAPE (IF ANY)
	AHEAD	ASTERN	PORT	ST'B'D		
FISHING						
TRAWLING						
NOT UNDER COMMAND						
RESTRICTED MANOEUVRABILITY						

4
SAFETY

Day Skippers are required to have a knowledge of the safety equipment which should be carried, its stowage and use. They must also be acquainted with fire precautions and fire fighting and the proper use of lifejackets and other personal safety equipment.

There are no legal requirements about safety equipment for yachts of under 45 ft (14.7m) overall length, but for craft below that size there is a set of recommendations drawn up by the RYA and approved by the Department of Trade & Industry. These divide pleasure boats into three categories, listing suitable equipment and precautions for each. The first two are applicable to the Day Skipper course. Bear in mind these are minimum recommendations.

Category 1 refers to vessels which will sail in daylight in estuaries and inshore waters close to a harbour.

Category 2 refers to vessels which cruise along the coast within 10 miles of land and within 4 hours sailing time of a safe refuge.

Yacht's Equipment

Auxiliary means of propulsion such as oars or paddles (Cat. 1)
Proper means of reefing the mainsail and a storm jib (Cat. 2)
Anchor appropriate to the size of vessel, complete with anchor warp of sufficient length for the area of operation and sufficiently strong anchor cleat or other fitting and stem fairlead (second anchor in the case of Cat. 2)
Manual bilge pump capable of discharging water over the side (Cat. 2)
Hand bailer (Cat. 1)
Two buckets with strong handles, fitted with lanyards (Cat. 2)

Radar reflector, mounted at least 10ft above sea level and as large as possible (Cat. 2)
Fixed navigation lights complying with the International Regulations For Preventing Collision At Sea (Cat. 2)
Powerful waterproof torch or Aldis lamp (Cat. 2)
Fog horn or other sound signalling apparatus for use in fog (Cat. 2)

Distress Flares

Minimum of 2 hand held red flares (4 for Cat. 2)
Two hand held orange smoke signals
Four hand held white flares (Cat. 2)
Two red parachute rockets (Cat. 2)

These need to be kept in a waterproof container and stowed in a dry place handy to the cockpit. All crews should be instructed where they are and how to use them. The safe life of these flares is usually three years. They all have expiry dates on them and must be safely disposed of after that time and fresh ones obtained. Opportunity should be found for lighting a flare yourself, perhaps during a practical course, so that you can do it with confidence if need arises.

Red flares are used for signal distress (i.e. that you are in serious danger). White flares are used to attract attention in emergency (e.g. to prevent a collision), not to signify distress. Orange smoke signals are an alternative to red flares and more easily seen in bright sunlight and by aircraft.

Fire Fighting Equipment (both categories)

Fire blanket for all craft carrying cooking equipment
Fire extinguishers of 1.5kg capacity, dry powder type
One must be fitted near the galley, the other near the engine compartment.

Craft with engines over 25 h.p. should have a fixed automatic or semi-automatic fire fighting system installed in the engine compartment.

The main fire hazards at sea are bottled gas and petrol, because their fumes are heavier than air and settle in the bilges. Precautions that can be taken are frequent ventilation of bilges and engine compartment, turning off tanks and cylinders when not in use and the fitting of a gas detector. Make sure all crew know siting of fire extingushers and how they operate. Suggest to smokers that they only do so on deck.

Fire fighting on a small boat is difficult because the source is often in an inaccessible space. Stop the vessel immediately and close hatches to reduce air flow. With a galley fire the fire blanket will be the first recourse. For engine and electrical fires use the extinguishers first. Never use water on fires involving liquids such as fuel or hot fat, nor on electrical fires, as the results can be explosive. You can use buckets of water on materials around these which may have caught fire, in order to prevent spreading and of course on fires from other causes like cigarette ends. Have the dinghy or liferaft prepared in case you have to abandon ship. As soon as it looks as if the fire may get out of control make a Mayday call or other distress signal.

Navigation and Radio

In both categories
Steering compass
Chart of sailing area
Tide tables

In category 2

Hand bearing compass
Chart of adjacent areas
Navigational instruments
Barometer
Clock or watch
Lead line or echo sounder
Navigational publications
*Radio receiver capable of picking up shipping forecasts on 200kHz
and the weather forecasts of local radio stations.*

General

Rigid or inflatable dinghy
Towing warp
Mooring warps and fenders
First aid kid (including seasickness tablets)
Engine and electrical spares
Bosun's bag with spare shackles and sail repair gear

Man Overboard Equipment

Horsehoe lifebelt fitted with drogue and self igniting light
Buoyant heaving line at least 30m length
Boarding ladder
Lifebelts should be kept on deck in proper racks so they can be thrown overboard quickly.

The buoyant line must be kept coiled on deck in a readily accessible place. Lights on life belts need checking to see they are in working order. Check the belts themselves regularly to see they can be freed easily.

Personal Safety

Adequate waterproof and warm clothing and seaboots for each person
Lifejacket or buoyancy aid for each person (Cat. 1)
Lifejacket for each person (Cat. 2)
Safety harnesses. (Cat. 2)

Lifejackets should be stowed in a dry, easily accessible place. It is the skippers responsibility to see that all on board know where they are, know how to get into and fasten them. The skipper must also decide when it is prudent that lifejackets should be worn by the crew on deck and see that they do. This will usually be at night, in fog, or at the onset of bad weather. Young children should wear them all the time on deck.

In bad weather or at night safety harnesses should be worn for changing or reefing sails or other jobs on the upper deck. Secure lifelines to clip on to should be rigged in good time.

Distress Signals by VHF

It is important to know the set procedures for making a VHF distress call so that in emergency it is done unhesitatingly and the message is received clearly. The internationally understood audio distress signal is MAYDAY and the equivalent of SOS in Morse. It is only used by a vessel which is in serious and imminent danger, or on behalf of one which is and unable to signal itself.

Distress calls are made on Channel 16. You broadcast the message, without waiting for anyone to reply to you, in the following manner.

Distress signal	'MAYDAY, MAYDAY, MAYDAY'
Name	'This is yacht Palmena, yacht Palmena, yacht Palmena'
Position	'Position One Nine Zero degrees, one mile from St Catherine's Point lighthouse'
Nature of distress	'Fire on board. Out of Control. Taking to liferaft'
Assistance required	'Require immediate assistance'
Other information to help rescue services	'Total crew two adults, one child. Blue hulled yacht
Invitation to reply	'Over'

If no reply is received the call should be repeated at intervals until you have some indication help is on its way.

Questions

1 How often should the red flares be renewed?
2 Where should the fire extinguishers be stowed?
3 What is the recommended clothing for sailing at sea during the early summer?
4 List 3 important items of navigational equipment.
5 When should safety harnesses be worn?

5

INTERNATIONAL REGULATIONS FOR PREVENTING COLLISIONS AT SEA

The International Regulations for Preventing Collisions at Sea are agreed by the maritime nations of the world. They apply to all vessels on the high seas which means as much to a yacht, however small, as to a supertanker. They also apply on all rivers and estuaries connected to the sea which are navigable by seagoing vessels. The Day Skipper candidate must know thoroughly rules 5, 7, 9 and 12–19 inclusive and to have a working knowledge of the remaining rules. They are naturally framed in exact legal language. It is tempting to try and paraphrase them, but there is no substitute for knowing the complete content. They are given here in full with comment and explanation as necessary.

Rule 5 Lookout

Every vessel shall at all times maintain a proper lookout by sight and hearing as well as by all available means appropriate in the prevailing circumstances and conditions so as to make a full appraisal of the situation and of the risk of collision.

As Skipper you are responsible for ensuring that a proper lookout is kept at all times. This will enable you to take appropriate action in plenty of time to avoid collision. A good look-out is always essential whether there are other vessels in the vicinity or not – for instance to avoid becoming entangled with a line of lobster pots.

Rule 7 Risk of Collision

a) *Every vessel shall use all available means appropriate to the prevailing circumstances and conditions to determine if risk of colli-*

sion exists. If there is any doubt such risk shall be deemed to exist.
b) *Proper use shall be made of radar equipment, if fitted and operational, to obtain early warning of risk of collision.*
c) *Assumptions shall not be made on the basis of scanty information, especially scanty radar information.*
d) *In determining if risk of collision exists the following considerations shall be among those taken into account:*
  i) such risk shall be deemed to exist if the compass bearing of an approaching vessel does not appreciably change
  ii) such risk may sometimes exist even when an appreciable bearing change is evident, particularly when approaching a very large vessel or a tow or when approaching a vessel at close range.

The skipper must check the compass bearing of an approaching vessel if there seems the slightest possibility that it may be on a converging course. If the bearing does not alter quickly and substantially the risk of collision must be deemed to exist. You will then have to decide which of you has the right of way and whether you have to give way or are the stand on vessel in the light of the subsequent rules. Remember that many ships, particularly cross-Channel car ferries and also many powered pleasure craft may be travelling at 20 knots or more, making the closing time in which action must be taken very short.

Rule 9 Narrow Channels

a) *A vessel proceeding along the course of a narrow channel or fairway shall keep as near to the outer limit of the channel or fairway which lies on her starboard side as is safe and practicable.*
b) *A vessel of less than 20m in length or a sailing vessel shall not impede the passage of a vessel which can safely navigate only within a narrow channel or fairway.*
c) *A vessel engaged in fishing shall not impede the passage of any other vessel navigating within a narrow channel or fairway.*
d) *A vessel shall not cross a narrow channel or fairway if such crossing impedes the passage of a vessel which can safely navigate only within such channel or fairway. The latter vessel may use the sound signal prescribed in Rule 34d if in doubt as to the intention of the crossing vessel.*

e) *In a narrow channel or fairway when overtaking can take place only if the vessel to be overtaken has to take action to permit safe passing, the vessel intending to overtake shall indicate her intention by sounding the appropriate signal prescribed in Rule 34c(i). The vessel to be overtaken shall, if in agreement, sound the appropriate signal prescribed in Rule 34c(ii) and take steps to permit safe passing. If in doubt she may sound the signals prescribed in Rule 34d.*

f) *A vessel nearing a bend or an area of narrow channel or fairway where other vessels may be obscured by an intervening obstruction shall navigate with particular alertness and caution and shall sound the appropriate signal prescribed in Rule 34e.*

g) *Any vessel shall, if the circumstances of the case admit, avoid anchoring in a narrow channel.*

So far as the yacht Skipper is concerned the essentials of Rule 9 are as follows:

Keep as far to the starboard side of the channel as conditions allow. Never anchor in a narrow channel or fairway unless circumstances force you to.
Keep out of the way of larger vessels which need the deep water. Never cross the channel in a way which will interfere with them. Don't fish in the fairway.

This rule also mentions sound signals laid down in a later section (Rule 34) and these are as follows:

5 short rapid blasts If you hear this be prepared to get out of the way quickly. It is made by a ship negotiating the fairway to indicate the captain is not sure what a craft crossing the channel is up to.

2 long 1 short blast Made by a vessel wishing to overtake another on its starboard side.

2 long 2 short Made by a vessel wishing to overtake another on its port side.

1 long 1 short 1 long 1 short Made by the ship to be overtaken if in agreement. She shall then take any necessary action to permit safe overtaking.

Rule 12 Sailing Vessels

a) *When two sailing vessels are approaching one another so as to involve risk of collision, one of them shall keep out of the way as follows:*

 i) When each has the wind on the different side, the vessel which has the wind on the port side shall keep out of the way of the other.

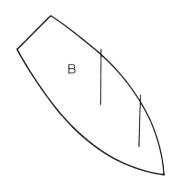

Wind

'A' keeps out of the way of 'B'

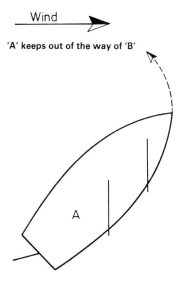

ii) When both have the wind on the same side the vessel which is to windward shall keep out of the way of the vessel which is to leeward.

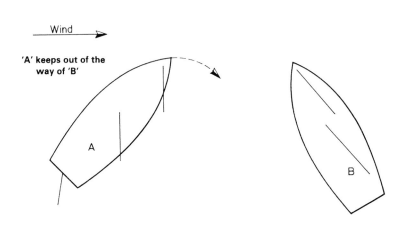

iii) If a vessel with the wind on the port side sees a vessel to windward and cannot determine with certainty whether the other vessel has the wind on the port or starboard side, she shall keep out of the way of the other.

b) *For the purposes of this rule the windward side shall be deemed to be the side opposite to that on which the mainsail is carried or, in the case of a square rigged vessel, the side opposite to that on which the largest fore and aft sail is carried.*

This is the rule you are likely to find yourself most frequently exercising in and around busy yachting ports so it is essential to be thoroughly familiar with it. Putting it into operation should become instinctive. On opposite tacks, starboard tack has right of way. On same tack, leeward boat has right of way.

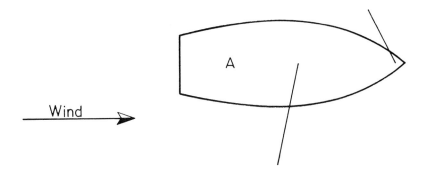

'B' keeps out of the way of 'A'

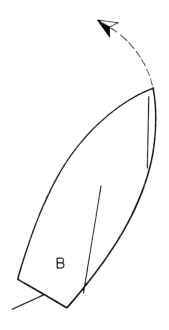

Yacht B finds herself governed by rule 12a(iii).
It is not clear whether Yacht A has the wind on
the starboard side so she keeps out of the way.

43

Rule 13 Overtaking

a) *Notwithstanding anything contained in the rules of this section, any vessel overtaking any other shall keep out of the way of the vessel being overtaken.*

b) *A vessel shall be deemed to be overtaking when coming up with another vessel from a direction more than 22.5° abaft her beam, that is, in such a position with reference to the vessel she is overtaking, that at night she would be able to see only the sternlight of that vessel but neither of her sidelights.*

c) *When a vessel is in any doubt as to whether she is overtaking another, she shall assume this is the case and act accordingly.*

d) *Any subsequent alteration of the bearing between the two vessels shall not make the overtaking vessel a crossing vessel within the meaning of these rules or relieve her of the duty of keeping clear of the overtaken vessel until she is finally past and clear.*

This overrides other considerations. Whenever you are overtaking in any situation the responsibility to keep clear becomes yours. That responsibility remains yours until you are well and truly clear of the overtaken vessel.

Rule 14 Head-on situation

a) *When two power driven vessels are meeting on reciprocal courses so as to involve risk of collision each shall alter her course to starboard so that each shall pass on the port side of the other.*

b) *Such a situation shall be deemed to exist when a vessel sees the other ahead or nearly ahead and by night she could see the masthead lights of the other in a line or nearly in a line and/or both sidelights and by day she observes the corresponding aspect of the other vessel.*

c) *When a vessel is in any doubt as to whether such a situation exists she shall assume that it does and act accordingly.*

This is the first rule dealing with power driven vessels, which means just as much a sailing yacht using her auxiliary engine even if the sails are still hoisted. When they are approaching each other head on or nearly head on both of them has to alter course so that they pass each other on their port sides.

Both 'A' and 'B' alter course to starboard

Rule 15 Crossing situation

When two power driven vessels are crossing so as to involve risk of collision, the vessel which has the other on her own starboard side shall keep out of the way and shall, if the circumstances of the case admit, avoid crossing ahead of the other vessel.

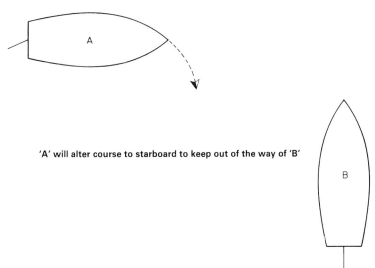

'A' will alter course to starboard to keep out of the way of 'B'

This rule governs the situation when powered craft are meeting in any situation other than head on. Again starboard has right of way. If when under engine you see another craft to your starboard you must keep clear. Never do it by trying to cross ahead of the other vessel unless there is no other way. Altering course is not the only way of keeping clear if you are the give way vessel. You could keep clear by reducing speed.

Rule 16 Action by Give-way vessel

Every vessel which is directed to keep out of the way of another vessel shall, so far as possible, take early and substantial action to keep well clear.

A short but important rule for all yacht skippers to understand. If it is not your right of way you are directed by this rule to take action in good time, not just rely on slipping under the other boat's stern at the last minute. And you are also required to make your alteration of course a more-than-adequate one. This not only ensures that you have done enough to avoid collision, but that it is made clear to the other vessel that you have taken avoiding action.

Rule 17 Action by Stand-on Vessel

a) *(i) Where one of two vessels is to keep out of the way the other shall keep her course and speed.*
ii) The latter vessel may however take action to avoid collision by her manoeuvre alone, as soon as it becomes apparent to her that the vessel required to keep out of the way is not taking appropriate action in compliance with these rules.
b) *When, from any cause, the vessel required to keep her course and speed finds herself so close that collision cannot be avoided by the action of the give-way vessel alone, she shall take such action as will best aid to avoid collision.*
c) *A power driven vessel which takes action in a crossing situation in accordance with sub-paragraph a(ii) of this rule to avoid collision with another power driven vessel shall, if the circumstances of the case admit, not alter course to port for a vessel on her own port side.*
d) *This Rule does not relieve the give way vessel of her obligation to keep out of the way.*

This rule makes it clear that when you have the right of way you are not absolved from all responsibility. First of all you must keep your vessel going on the same course and speed until all danger of collision has passed. If someone else has altered course to avoid you it may confuse them if your heading suddenly changes, or you slow down. You may think you are helping, but your duty is to go 'steady as you are'. Secondly you must be constantly alert to the movements of the give-way vessel. If you find she is not giving way in time and you are getting close, the responsibility becomes yours to avoid collision in the best way you can. If this situation arises size it up in good time and be positive. Don't hesitatingly alter course first one way then the other.

Rule 18 Responsibilities between Vessels

Except where Rules 9, 10 and 13 otherwise require:
a) *A power driven vessel underway shall keep out of the way of:*
   i) A vessel not under command;
   ii) A vessel restricted in her ability to manoeuvre;
   iii) A vessel engaged in fishing;
   iv) A sailing vessel
b) *A sailing vessel shall keep out of the way of:*
   i) A vessel not under command;
   ii) A vessel restricted in her ability to manoeuvre;
   iii) A vessel engaged in fishing.
c) *A vessel engaged in fishing when underway shall, so far as possible, keep out of the way of:*
   i) A vessel not under command;
   ii) A vessel restricted in her ability to manoeuvre.
d) *i) Any vessel other than a vessel not under command or a vessel restricted in her ability to manoeuvre shall, if the circumstances of the case admit, avoid impeding the safe passage of a vessel constrained by her draught, exhibiting the signals in Rule 28.*
   ii) A vessel constrained by her draught shall navigate with particular caution having full regard to her special condition.

Rule 18 looks complicated but is important to grasp as it covers relationships with all types of other craft, particularly in the situation where you are most likely to meet most of them, going in and out of harbour. **18b** is especially important as it tells the sailing yacht skipper what other craft he should keep out of the way of, unless there is anything to the contrary in rules 9, 10 and 13. Many people still have the idea that 'power gives way to sail', but although the old rule made in the last century when steam ships were first coming in is still embodied in **18a** there are exceptions as laid down in **18b**. A vessel not under command (that is to say unable to make way or manoeuvre) may not be readily identifiable, but should be displaying a special signal specified in a later rule. A vessel restricted in ability to manoeuvre could be any large ship in a narrow channel, or a dredger or cable laying vessel, or a deep laden vessel 'constrained by her draught' in waters which may not seem shallow to you but are to her. Notwithstanding the rules most yachtsmen out for pleasure prefer to surrender right of way to working craft, but they should always make their intention plain by altering course early and substantially.

Day Skipper students are expected to have a working knowledge of the remaining rules which mainly concern the lights to be shown by vessels, sound signals and distress signals. The more important provisions are summarised here.

Lights for sailing vessels

A sailing vessel over 20 metres underway at night must display red and green (port and starboard) sidelights and a white sternlight.

Under 20 metres the red and green lights may be in a combined lantern at the bows, with a separate sternlight. Alternately a combined tricolour lantern may be used at the mast head visible all round and displaying red, green and white sectors.

A sailing craft under 7 metres is not required to show lights all the time but must have a white light available to display to prevent collision.

Lights for power vessels

A vessel over 50 metres long under way at night displays red and green port and starboard lights and two white masthead lights. Below 50 metres there is only one masthead light.

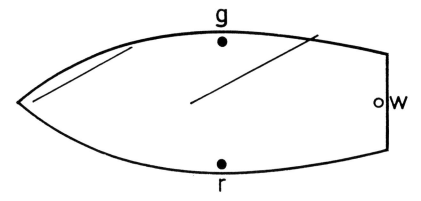

A sailing vessel at night must carry the lights shown above, but if under 20 metres has alternative options.

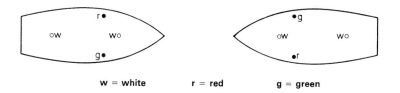

w = white   r = red   g = green

Identifying a head on situation at night. Each would see the red and green lights of the other and alter course to starboard.

A motor yacht under 20 metres must show a combined red and green lantern at the bows, a white masthead light and a white sternlight. Below 12 metres the masthead and stern lights may be combined in one all-round light.

A motor boat of less than 7 metres travelling at less than 7 knots may show one all-round white light.

A sailing yacht is required if motoring to hoist on the forestay or other convenient place, a cone pointing downwards.

Sound signals

These are only given in clear weather and not to be confused with the fog signals.

1 short blast = I am altering course to starboard
2 short blasts = I am altering course to port
3 short blasts = I am going astern
5 or more short blasts may mean that somebody is signalling you to get out of the way.

These signals are usually given by larger working vessels manoeuvring in the vicinity of other craft. They are not generally given by yachts. The rules do however require that every vessel of less than 12 metres shall have the means to make an efficient sound signal in poor visibility.

Distress signals

The regulations list 14 different ways of summoning help in emergencies. Many of them are not relevant to small boat sailing. Those that are are listed below.

SOS by torch in the Morse code ··· ‒‒‒ ···

'MAYDAY' by voice on the radio telephone.

Red hand flare or rocket parachute flare.

Orange smoke signal.

Slow and repeated raising and lowering of outstretched arms.

Questions

1 Which vessel keeps out of the way when the wind is on different sides?
2 Which vessel keeps out of the way when the wind is on the same side?
3 What happens if you are not sure whether the other vessel has the wind on the port side or the starboard side?
4 How can you tell if you are the overtaking vessel?
5 If two power driven vessels are meeting end on what does each do?
6 When two power driven vessels are crossing which vessel keeps out of the way?
7 If you are stand on vessel what do you have to do?
8 If you are the stand on vessel can you take any action to avoid collision?
9 What four vessels does a power driven vessel give way to?
10 If you are in a sailing vessel what other vessels do you have to keep out of the way of?
11 In restricted visibility what do the Rules say about the speed of vessels?
12 If you hear a fog signal forward of your beam what should you do?

6
NAVIGATIONAL TERMS

Although the Day Skipper may not be making very long passages and have no intention of being out of sight of land a basic knowledge of navigation is nevertheless essential. Finding your way at sea is not like motoring on land. It is more analogous to walking over mountains or wild moorland country. There are no signposts, nobody to ask the way and an attendant risk of deteriorating conditions. Therefore even on the shortest voyage you need to know just where you are and how to find your way from there.

Before we can begin to consider the ways of doing this it is necessary to understand a few of the special words used in navigation.

Latitude and Longitude

Lines of latitude run round the earth (only in theory of course) parallel with the equator. Lines of longitude run round the earth the other way and are different insofar as they all pass through the north and south poles and so converge instead of staying parallel. Their use to the navigator is that they provide a set of co-ordinates for referring to any point on the surface of the globe.

To provide these co-ordinates latitude and longitude are measured in degrees. The earth is treated as a circle and it is as if you have placed a protractor in the centre of it and marked off the degrees on the perimeter of the circle. Starting from the equator which is 0 degrees, latitude is measured north and south of that point up to 90 degrees at the poles. Longitude is measured in both directions from the Prime Meridian, the 0 degree line which runs through Greenwich, up to 180 degrees which runs through the middle of the Pacific Ocean and is the International Date Line. Latitudes are thus expressed as so many degrees north or so many degrees south, meaning north or south of the equator. Longitudes are expressed as so many degrees east or west, according to which side of the Greenwich meridian. To be able to pinpoint a position with more accuracy the degrees are divided into minutes and seconds. There are 60 minutes in each degree and 60 seconds in each minute. Latitude and longitude are shown on charts along the edges and so can be used as co-ordinates (crossed lines) to show a position anywhere on it.

For example Beachy Head lighthouse is in latitude 50 degrees 44 minutes north and longitude 0 degrees 14 minutes 6 seconds east. This would be expressed simply as 50°44′N 0° 14.6′E. The latitude is always given first.

The scale of chart generally used for coastal cruising shows divisions equal to fifths of a nautical mile, making it possible to give a position to one decimal point as in the example above.

Position

A navigator needs always to know the position of the ship and to plot it on the chart. He must also know how to tell someone else that position, especially if in emergency he is in touch with rescue services by radio. It can be expressed by latitude and longitude as seen above. Or it can be given as a compass bearing and distance off, as discussed later.

The navigator recognises different kinds of position. These are:

Fixed Position (fix for short). One obtained by cross bearings or other methods, or by electronic aids, and giving the best degree of certainty.

Dead Reckoning Position (DR for short). A position marked on the chart which takes account of the course the vessel has steered and the distance travelled since the last fixed position. It is simply where you reckon you are and will only be relied on when there are no better means of determining position (no headland on which to take a bearing, etc.).

Estimated Position (EP) A step better than DR because it includes taking into account the effect of tidal set and leeway as well as course and distance travelled.

Bearings

A bearing is a compass direction from your vessel to some other vessel or object. Those of a fixed identified object have many uses in navigation as we shall see in later sections. Two or more bearings can be used to plot a fixed position on a chart. If you are giving your position to somebody else in emergency one bearing of an object which you can name (say a lighthouse or headland) plus the estimated distance you are from it will do. All bearings taken with a compass are magnetic bearings because the compass needle points to the magnetic north pole. For navigational purposes this will need to be converted to a true bearing. Any true bearing you have taken from a chart or pilot book will need to be converted to magnetic to give the helmsman a course to steer.

Almost all modern yacht compasses are notated from 0 to 360 degrees starting and finishing at north, so all bearings are expressed as a number of degrees. Traditional compasses, still to be encountered on old vessels, are noted in 32 'points', each equivalent to 11.25 degrees and named north-west, west-north-west, etc instead of numbered.

Course

This is the direction (expressed as a true compass bearing) in which you wish to go. It may not be the course you are actually steering at the moment. Because of the effects of wind, tide and compass differences you may have to compensate by steering on a different compass heading. What you have actually achieved at the end of a given period will be called the 'course made good'.

Distance

This is measured at sea in nautical miles. A nautical mile is equal to one minute of latitude and can be measured off on the chart as described in a later chapter. It is about 2,000 yards or 1,853 metres, which is rather longer than the land mile of 1,760 yards. Most modern yachts have an instrument known as a log with a dial showing the distance travelled. Before these were widely available the most common device of which many are still in use was Walker's Patent Log which was streamed astern and registered on a dial clamped inboard.

Whatever kind of log is used it is important to remember that what they show is the distance covered through the water. Because of the flow of tide past the boat this may be more or less than the distance you have actually travelled over the ground and the difference must be taken into consideration when navigating.

Knots

A knot is a measurement of speed at sea. One knot is one nautical mile per hour. If you are sailing at four miles an hour you would say your speed was four knots. To say 'four knots an hour' would be meaningless. The term derived from the days when speed was measured by streaming a knotted line astern from a reel and counting the number of knots run out in a given time.

Questions

1 By what unit is distance measured at sea?
2 What is the definition of a knot?
3 What is the difference between DR and EP?
4 Describe two methods of giving someone else your position.
5 What is a fix?

7

NAVIGATIONAL CHARTS AND PUBLICATIONS

The Day Skipper needs to be able to use charts and other publications for navigation. This section of the syllabus is to help you become familiar with them before learning how to use them.

Charts

The main producers of charts are the Admiralty who publish them for all parts of the world. For the popular yachting area there are also two commonly used commercially published charts, Stanfords and Imray. These are a little more simplified and with more colour. These often have some course lines, compass bearings and distances already printed on them which can save some navigation work. The Admiralty also produce practice charts for shore based students. These must never be used for navigation.

Like maps charts come in different scales. The largest scale are harbour charts which show the entrance and approach of just one port. A smaller scale might show, for instance, the whole western end of the English Channel. This is known as a passage chart. Intermediate scales would show a particular stretch of coastline. You must have charts covering the whole area in which you intend sailing and it would be wise to carry charts of adjacent areas. Many Stanford charts have harbour plans printed on the reverse with information about their approaches.

Admiralty charts are sold by appointed agents, usually a yacht chandler and can be chosen from a catalogue with index maps. Most chandlers stock the commercial charts.

Information on Charts

Charts carry a wealth of information which you must learn to interpret. These are some of the more important.

DEPTHS IN METRES

SCALE 1:200 000 at lat 50°00′N

Depths are in metres reduced approximately to Lowest Astronomical Tide.

Heights are in metres. Underlined figures are drying heights, in metres and decimetres, above Chart Datum; all other heights are above Mean High Water Springs

Projection: Mercator. Positions are based on the Ordnance Survey of Great Britain (1936) Datum.

Authorities: Hydrography is taken from British and French Government surveys to 1971. The topography is taken chiefly from the Ordnance Survey and the Institut Géographique National.

CROSS-CHANNEL POWER CABLE

Mariners are warned not to anchor or trawl in the vicinity of the cross-Channel power cable, and on no account to cut this cable should it be fouled.

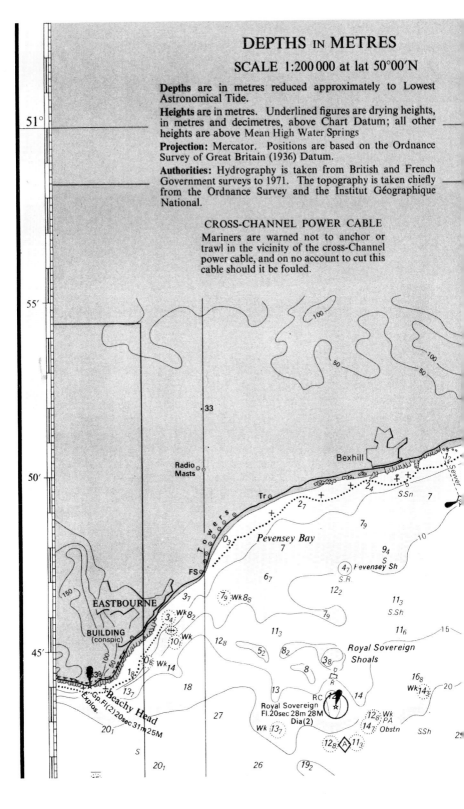

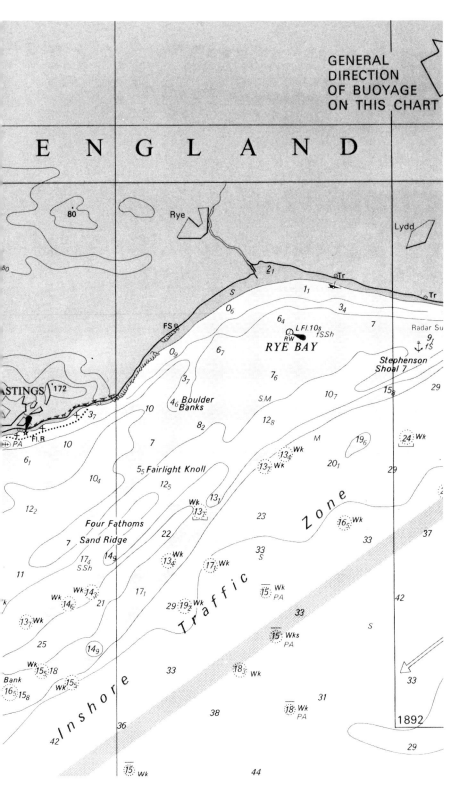

Depth of water. This is shown both by contour lines and by figures at a vast number of points. These may be in fathoms and feet or in metres and tenth of a metre. (A fathom is a traditional measure now going out of use and equals six feet.) It is essential to look (usually in one corner of the chart) to see which before you start using it. The depth shown is not the depth of water you will find there except on rare occasions. It is a theoretical depth based on a point known as chart datum from which you will be able to calculate the depth of water at that point for any given time by using your tide tables.

Dangers. Rocks, shoals, wrecks, etc are marked with conventional signs. The Admiralty publishes a book called 'Symbols and Abbreviations Used On Admiralty Charts', Ref. No. 5011, which gives all conventional signs used on charts and is worth studying.

Aids to navigation. All lighthouses, daymarks, buoys and prominent buildings or other shoreline features which will be useful for the navigator to fix a position by with bearings.

Nature of the bottom. Shows what the sea bottom is like, an important consideration when you are choosing an anchorage. Usually given as an abbreviation such as s. for sand, sh. for shingle, etc.

Tidal streams. Admiralty charts show at intervals a diamond shape containing a letter. The letters refer to a table to be found at the top or bottom of the chart which gives the strength and direction of tidal stream for each hour of the tide. From this information the navigator can work out what effect the tide will have on the course he has planned.

Direction. Every chart has one or more representations of the compass printed on them. This is commonly known as the 'compass rose'. They will show true north, magnetic north at the time of publication and the annual rate at which the variation between true and magnetic north is increasing or decreasing. The navigator uses the compass rose to either (a) transfer a compass bearing to his position line or (b) transfer a course line plotted on the chart to the compass rose so that he knows what compass heading to steer. This is usually done with a set of parallel rules.

Distance. The chart also has a scale of distance which the navigator uses to measure his progress. It is the latitude scale along the right and left hand sides of the chart, divided into minutes which represent a nautical mile. Measurements are made by opening the points of a pair of dividers over the distance to be measured (say from a buoy you have just passed to the harbour entrance) and then laying the points (taking care they do not move) on the latitude scale.

It is important to use only the latitude scale because minutes of longitude are not equal to a nautical mile. It is also important to use the latitude scale of the chart you are on. Due to the distortion inherent in representing a round earth on flat paper, the value would be different a long way north or south of your position.

Navigational Publications

As well as charts it is necessary to become familiar with a number of other navigation publications.

Nautical almanacs. These are published annually and contain tide tables for a large number of principal ports around the coast, together with other tidal information, lists of lighthouses, radio beacons and other navigational aids, and a huge amount of other valuable information. The best known is *Reed's* and is long established. More recently there has appeared the *Macmillan Silk Cut Almanac* which has been devised solely for yachtsman and contains more pilotage information applicable to yachting ports.

Pilot books. These are guides to different areas of coastline giving information about dangerous areas, the safety or otherwise of different harbours and anchorages in different conditions and advising on the safe approach to them. There are Admiralty pilots written for shipping and not really suitable for the coastal yachtsmen, but there are a number of commercially published pilot books specially for yachtsmen, each devoted one popular cruising area. They make a helpful supplement to the navigator's knowledge but must not be used as a substitute for adequate chartwork.

Tidal atlases. The Admiralty publish a number of these for different areas. They show by means of arrows the speed and direction of the tidal set, there being a page for every hour before and after high water. Many people find them easier to use than the tidal stream diamonds and tables on the charts and though this is a less accurate way of working it may not be significant on a short coastal voyage. They are certainly quicker for obtaining an overall picture of tidal movement.

Chart Correction. Charts become out of date. Because of the safety factors involved this matters rather more than with a land map and they must be up-dated regularly. To make this possible the Admiralty publish *Notices To Mariners* weekly, containing the information which seafarers need to correct their charts. They include such information as a change in the position of a buoy, a new wreck which has been marked as a danger to navigation, a change in the lights displayed by a lighthouse or a sandbank which has moved.

There is a special quarterly edition of *Notices To Mariners* containing only the changes important to small boat users and it is advisable to make use of this. The alternative is to take your charts back to the chart agent for correction, for which there will be a charge.

When you buy a chart look at the bottom left hand corner and see the date it was printed and the date last corrected. Make your subsequent corrections in indelible mauve ink and note the date of them at the bottom left hand corner.

Charts should be stored flat whenever possible. If you keep them on a chart table protect them when not in use from coffee stains and other damage by a sheet of plastic or cardboard. In a boat too small for a chart table where you may need to use them in the cockpit, make an adequate clear plastic cover.

Questions

1 What are the Admiralty Notices to Mariners used for?
2 Where do you find the number of a chart?
3 Where do you measure distance from on a chart?
4 What information do tidal atlases give you?
5 What is the purpose of the compass rose?

Exercises

1 Draw a course from a position 2 miles south of Dungeness Light-house to a position 2 miles south of Beachy Head Lighthouse. Measure the distance.
2 Find the course from 1 mile north of the Royal Sovereign Light-vessel to Rye Bay Buoy. What is the distance?
3 Find the true course from the yellow buoy in Pevensey Bay to the Royal Sovereign Lightvessel. What is the distance?

8

NAVIGATIONAL DRAWING INSTRUMENTS

It is necessary to be familiar with the simple instruments used in chartwork, and to practice with them so that they can be handled with confidence. Otherwise it can be difficult at times to cope on the chart table of a small boat at sea.

Parallel Rules

These are used for laying off a course or a bearing on the chart. They look like two rulers that have been fastened together side by side, with an arm to move on.

Suppose you have drawn on the chart the course you wish to travel from your point of departure to your destination. If you lay the parallel rules along this line and then 'walk' them to the nearest compass rose on the chart, until one edge is passing through the centre of the rose, you will be able to read off the compass course you need to make good in order to arrive.

When laying a bearing of an object on the chart the same principle applies, but in reverse. Lay the rules on the compass rose against the compass bearing you have taken, then walk the rules across the chart until they pass through the object of which you have taken the bearing. You can then draw the line of the bearing on the chart.

Always when using parallel rules take care that you read off the course on the compass rose in the correct direction and not in the reciprocal. An alternative to using the compass rose is to read off a course by using the gradations etched on the rules against a line of longitude on the chart, but most people find it much easier to use the compass rose where the course can be read off directly.

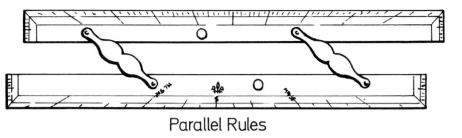

Parallel Rules

Douglas Protractor

For most small boat work a 15 ins pair of rules is adequate. An alternative pattern preferred by some is the roller variety which you roll instead of walk across the chart.

Douglas Protractor

There are on the market a number of proprietary plotting instruments of which the Douglas Protractor is the most popular. It consists of a square of transparent plastic with a hole in the centre and is marked in degrees round the edges. It can be used to lay off bearings on the chart but because of its size it is not so satisfactory for laying off courses.

Dividers

Dividers are used to measure distance on the chart. If you want to see how far it is from one point to another, open out the points of the dividers to stretch between them, then lay the points on the latitude scale at the side of the chart. Conversely, if you are sailing at four knots and want to see where you will be if you continue at the same course and speed for the next hour you would measure off four miles with the divider points at the side of the chart and then mark off the distance on your course line.

It pays to have a good pair of dividers. The bow shaped type are easier and more reliable to handle for chartwork than the straight sided sort used for school geometry.

Pencils and Rubbers

Soft pencils are best because they do not damage the chart and rub out easily. Hard pencils cut in and are difficult to erase and you will want to use the same chart over and over again. About 2B is right. A large soft eraser is also needed.

9
COMPASSES

The compass is the most important instrument on the boat and a good understanding of its use is essential. Its accuracy is influenced by two factors which have to be taken into account by the navigator. They are known as 'variation' and 'deviation'.

Variation

Because the compass needle is magnetic it follows the earth's magnetic field and rarely points to true geographical north, but to the magnetic north pole. The angle between the two is called variation. The variation can be to either east or west of true north and will also vary in amount according to where you are on the surface of the earth. It is not constant and will either increase or decrease a little each year. In the English Channel at the moment variation is about 6 degrees west of true north and is decreasing at the rate of about 8 minutes annually.

All Admiralty charts have printed on the compass rose the amount of variation for the year the chart was published, together with the annual rate of change, so from this information the current variation can be quickly calculated. For coastal sailing it may be safely assumed that the variation will remain fixed throughout the area being covered and the value calculated from the nearest compass rose can be used all the time. For long ocean voyages the information is obtained from a special Admiralty chart showing the magnetic variation for the whole surface of the earth.

When laying off courses on the chart and when taking bearings magnetic variation must always be allowed for.

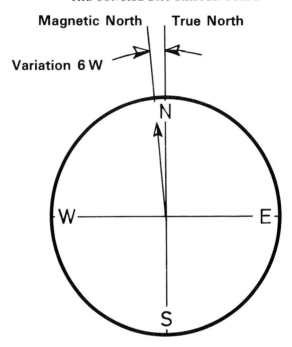

Deviation

The compass is also affected by any metallic object with a ferrous content which may be nearby, or by electric wiring. This is known as deviation and it too causes a deflection of the needle away from true north. Engines, yacht fittings and hull fastenings can all be guilty of causing deviation, as can such objects as a knife worn by a helmsman. Beer cans used to be a problem but nowadays most of them are non-ferrous. If you are careful about where offending objects are placed the amount of deviation found in small yachts of wood or glass fibre will be small. Steel hulls are more susceptible as they become magnetised by the earth's magnetic field, especially if laid up facing in one direction for any lengthy period.

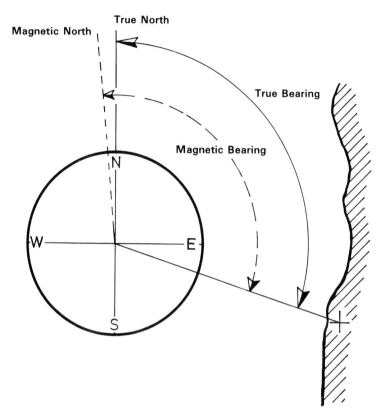

A bearing taken of the object on the shore marked by a cross illustrates the difference between true and magnetic bearings. The compass will show a reading of the angle between the bearing line and magnetic north, but the true bearing will be the angle between the line and true north.

Working Out Deviation

Any deviation has to be applied to the correction of compass courses, along with variation. Unfortunately its value cannot be found by reference to the chart as with variation, and the skipper must work it out for himself, unless he can afford a professional compass adjuster to do the job for him. Deviation is further complicated by the fact that it is not a constant figure, but varies according to which way the boat is heading.

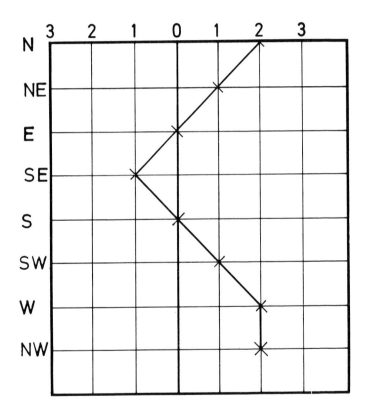

Example of deviation card plotted by swinging the compass.

The process by which the deviation is worked out is known as 'swinging the compass'. It is done by lining up two objects on the shore to provide a transit and comparing the bearing of this transit as shown on your compass with a true bearing taken off the chart. It is necessary to do this with the boat's head pointing in different directions until you have been right round in a circle. This can be done by anchoring and having someone tow the stern round with the dinghy. A comparison should be made at intervals of every 45 degrees or less and the deviation on that heading noted.

In large vessels which have compasses mounted in binnacles it is possible to correct or minimise the deviation discovered when swinging the compass by the strategic arrangement of a number of small iron bars. As this is not possible on small boats it is the practice to draw up a chart or graph which shows at a glance the amount and direction of deviation for every compass heading. The skipper then refers to this when working out true bearings and courses. Such cards are often inherited from previous owners when purchasing a yacht, but if not one should be made as soon as possible. It is wise to swing the compass afresh at the start of every sailing season, as gear which affects the compass may well have been moved about during the winter lay-up.

It is also possible to find deviation by taking a compass bearing of the sun at sunrise or sunset. There are tables in the nautical almanacs which give the true bearing of the sun at sunrise and sunset in different latitudes in particular days of the year. The difference between this bearing and true east or west is known as the amplitude. The difference between your compass bearing of the sun and the true bearing given in the almanac will give you the deviation, after an adjustment has been made for variation.

Application of Variation and Deviation

Since both variation and deviation affect the compass the sum of the two must be applied by the navigator to obtain a true reading. The combination of the two is known as **compass error**.

Compass error will have a value either west or east of true north. If the variation and the deviation both have a westerly value then they must be added together to give the compass error. If one is easterly and the other westerly they must be subtracted and the lesser value taken from the greater. For example:

variation 6 degrees W + deviation 2 degrees W = compass error 8°W.
variation 6 degrees W − deviation 2 degrees E = compass error 4°W.

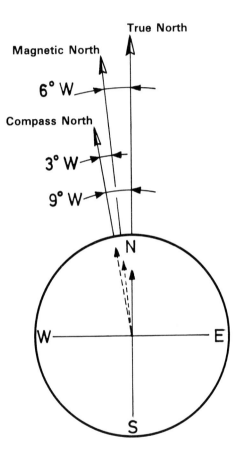

Combination of variation and deviation makes up compass error.

True bearings and courses

Only true bearings and courses are laid off on a chart. All compass bearings must be converted to true bearings, and all true courses which are laid off on the chart must be converted to compass courses for the helmsman to steer by.

When making a passage the true courses should be laid off on the chart before leaving harbour and should be double checked to make sure that no error has occurred and that they are safe. The true course should be written on the chart by the course line, together with the compass course to be steered. The distance along that particular leg of the course should also be noted.

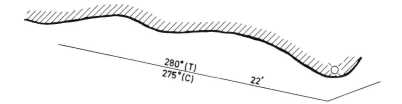

True courses (T) should be laid off on the chart and converted to compass courses (C) for the helmsman to steer.

If there is no deviation it is possible to use the magnetic compass rose on the chart to lay off courses and bearings, but care must be taken not to confuse true and compass north. If the compass rose is not used, a bearing must be converted to true before laying off.

There is a nemonic to help with the conversion. When converting from a true course to a compass course remember TELC.

T	E	L	C
True	East	Left	Compass

If the error is easterly apply the correction to the left of north, ie subtract the error. If the error is westerly then apply the correction to the right, ie add the error. If you are sailing in British waters then at the moment the error should always be added when converting a true course to a compass course, unless you have an unusually large easterly deviation.

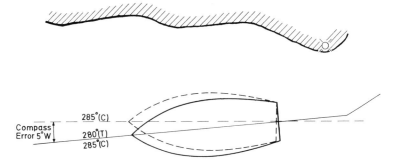

The yacht above is steering a course of 285° to make good a true course of 280°, there being compass error (variation + deviation) of 5°.

If you are converting a compass bearing to a true bearing the nemonic is CERT

C	E	R	T
Compass	East	Right	True

If the error is easterly apply the correction to the right of north, ie add the error. If the error is westerly apply the correction to the left of north, ie subtract the error. Again, it is usual to subtract the compass error when converting a compass bearing into a true bearing in British waters.

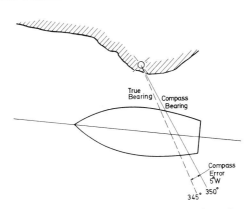

This yacht has taken a compass bearing of 350°, but with compass error of 5°W the true bearing to be laid off on the chart is 345°.

Examples Variation 6°W deviation 1°E. If the true course is 045 what is the compass course?

Variation 6°W minus deviation 1°E = compass error 5°W

Compass error W therefore add (TELC)

True course 045° plus compass error 5°W = course to steer 050°

Variation 4°W deviation 2°W. If the compass bearing was 257° what is the true bearing to lay off on the chart?

Variation 4°W plus deviation 2°W = compass error 6°W

Compass error W therefore subtract (CERT)

Compass bearing 257° minus compass error 6°W = true bearing 251°

Use of Hand Bearing Compass

Only on large vessels is it possible to take accurate bearings with the steering compass. Then it is usually fitted with a metal ring round the top to facilitate sighting. The compass of a small boat is generally fixed too low down in the boat to enable a sight to be taken from it, or is mounted on a cockpit bulkhead with no all-round view. Consequently yachts should carry a hand bearing compass, which as its name implies is held in the hand for the particular purpose of taking bearings. This needs a secure stowage handy to the cockpit. It will be subject to the same influences as the steering compass and will have its own deviation, so its accuracy on different headings must be checked and noted.

Siting of Steering Compass

The positioning of the steering compass is important. With a new yacht you may be asked to say where you want it fixed or you may have to think of repositioning one in an older yacht. As we have seen a position that avoids too much deviation is essential. Apart from that it must be fixed in a position where the helmsman can easily see it. Make sure that it is fixed so that the 'lubber line' along the face of the compass card is in line with the fore and aft centre line of your vessel. Many compasses have a light built in for night sailing, but if not see that the compass is placed where it can be illuminated. It needs only a subdued light otherwise it may spoil the helmsman's night vision which can be dangerous.

Questions

1 What is the compass error if the variation is 5°W and the deviation is 3°E?
2 What is the compass error if the variation is 7°W and the deviation is 2°W?
3 What is the compass course to steer if the variation is 5°W and the deviation is 1°E for a true course of 160°?
4 What is the true bearing to lay off on the chart if the compass bearing is 075°. The variation is 6°W and the deviation 0°?
5 Summarise briefly how you would find the deviation of a yachts' compass.

10
CHARTWORK

A skipper must at all times know the position of the vessel on the chart. By this means he or she not only keeps track of the vessel's progress, but is aware of any dangers to navigation which might be ahead or become hazards in the case of a shift of wind. In practice chartwork in a small boat is not easy. Many of them lack the luxury of an adequate sized chart table on which to work and the motion of the boat makes accurate plotting difficult. This makes it all the more important that chartwork is practised on shore so that you are thoroughly familiar with the methods and can exercise the skills with confidence at sea, even if you are feeling queasy.

Leaving Harbour

Before leaving harbour the courses for your planned voyage should be drawn on the chart. See chapter on passage planning.

As soon as you are well clear of the harbour and its traffic and in a position to think of heading in the direction you wish to go, say a mile or so offshore, you should take a fix of your position (the methods are dealt with in the next chapter). For navigation purposes this is your 'point of departure', not the harbour you left. When leaving harbours you are concentrating on other traffic and on the buoys marking the deep water channels and probably altering course frequently. You may need to look at the chart to see how the entrance is marked, but there is no need to do any plotting on it. Chartwork begins with the point of departure.

Dead Reckoning Position

The simplest method of keeping track of your progress is by marking your dead reckoning position (DR) on the chart at regular intervals. As we have seen this is simply a combination of course steered and distance travelled as shown by the log. If the steering has been good and the log accurate it will give you a fair approximation of your position to be used between intervals of obtaining a more reliable position or when for any reason (such as bad visibility) a position is not obtainable. Write time beside each mark.

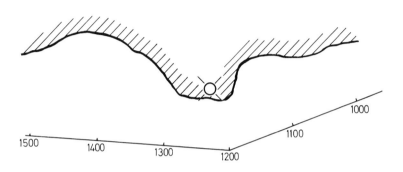

DR positions laid off along a course line.

Estimated Position

An estimated position (EP) is one which, in addition to course and distance travelled, takes into account the ship's leeway and the speed and direction (known as the 'set') of the tidal stream. It is not wholly accurate as a means of telling position because it is difficult to estimate leeway with any certainty and the tidal data is only an approximation. Nevertheless EP is more likely to be right than DR and should be plotted on the chart at regular intervals, marking the time and the letters EP against it.

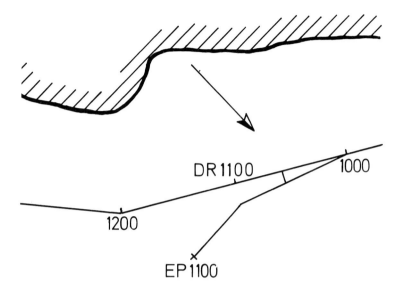

The yacht leaves the first position at 1000 with a north westerly wind allowing 5° for leeway. The leeway or wake course is plotted for the distance sailed in the first hour. But she has been helped on her way by a south-west flowing tidal current, so that is then added to give an EP at 1100.

Allowing for Leeway

Leeway is the term used for the way in which a yacht is set down wind from the course she actually appears to be heading on. The amount of leeway will depend on the strength of the wind and the point of sailing the boat is on (it is most when close hauled and minimal when running). The amount of leeway also differs from yacht to yacht according to her design. One with a high superstructure and shallow draught will make more leeway than a deep keeled yacht with little superstructure. A skipper must become familiar with the leeway characteristics of his own boat and allow for it when setting a course and working out an EP. Leeway is always expressed in degrees. The best way of judging it is by looking astern and observing your wake, estimating the angle by which this differs from the fore and aft line of the yacht. You may find it helpful to use a hand bearing compass to help you judge the angle more accurately.

The amount of leeway must be added or subtracted to your true course to determine what compass course you must steer. As you will see from the diagram below a yacht with a true course of 80° in a southerly wind and making leeway of 10° would need to steer a compass course of 90° in order to make good her intended course. This course corrected for leeway is known as the 'wake course'. If, in the example shown, the wind were from the north the leeway would need to be subtracted and a course of 70° steered to make good a true course of 80°.

Leeway is always applied to the true course after allowance has been made for tide which will be dealt with now.

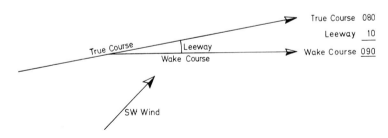

A course having allowed for leeway is called a wake course.

Allowing for Tidal Stream

Everybody is familiar with the rise and fall of the tide against the shore. What is not so clearly pictured by most of us is the flow of the tide out at sea where it sets up a complex pattern of streams or currents which are constantly changing in strength and direction throughout the tidal cycle. Although the speed of these streams may seem small, ranging as a rule between 0.5 and 2 knots, they can make a big difference to small boat navigation. While a big ship steaming at 20 knots may not be much inconvenienced by a 2 knot tide a yachtsman sailing at 4 knots with an adverse 2 knot tide is obviously going to take twice as long to get home as he thought.

A tidal stream flowing directly against you will effectively reduce your speed by an amount equal to its own rate of flow. You will be sailing just as fast through the water, but making progress more slowly over the ground. Conversely a stream flowing in your direction of travel will move you along faster, adding its own speed to your sailing speed. In many instances however the stream will be at an angle to your course line, deflecting you from it. In this case you will have to calculate the compass course the helmsman must steer to overcome this. The examples below show how this is done.

The information you need to do this at sea will come from the tidal diamonds on the chart or from a tidal atlas. The amount of deflection from course caused by the tide is called the 'set'. Tidal streams are always referred to by the direction in which they are going (i.e. a south west stream is flowing towards the south west). This is unlike the wind which we always refer to by the direction from which it is coming.

The knowledge in the above section is used both to plot an EP and to work out the compass course to steer in order to sail your desired true course.

Examples The course you are trying to make is 230° (T) and the tidal stream is setting 290° at 2 knots. What is the course to steer to counteract that tidal stream? Vessel's speed 4 knots.

Line AC represents the true course to steer 230°

Line AB represents the tidal stream 290° at 2 knots

Line BC represents the course to steer allowing for the effect of the tidal stream.

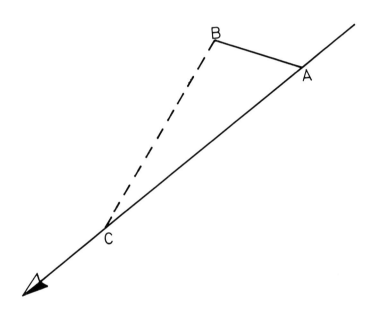

From the departure point lay off the direction of the tidal stream. Then with compasses or dividers, open to a radius of the vessel's speed in knots, in this case 4 knots, make an arc on line AC. Join B and C to give course to steer allowing for tidal stream. Sometimes with a small scale chart it may be necessary to double the tide scale and double the vessel's speed. Now let us try the same problem with leeway.

The true course you are trying to make is 040°. The current is setting 110° at 1.5 knots. The wind is north west force 5. Find the course to steer allowing for current and leeway. The vessel makes 10° of leeway. Vessel's speed 4 knots.

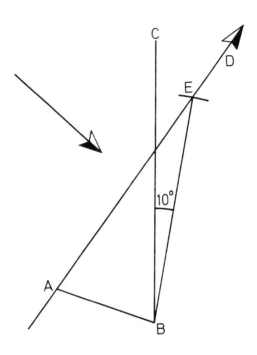

Line AD represents true course, angle CBE represents leeway, line AB represents tidal stream and line BC represents course to steer to counteract leeway and current. In this case both wind and tide are setting you in a south-easterly direction.

Plotting fixes

In addition to plotting your progress by DR and EP it is wise at intervals during any passage to obtain a 'fix' – that is to plot your position more accurately by means of observation. With modern technology there are many instruments which will give instant positions by latitude and longitude which can be transferred to the chart. Even if you are fortunate enough to possess one of these it is essential that you know how to obtain a fix with hand compass bearings using one or more of the traditional methods. It is not easy taking accurate bearings in a small boat which may be rolling about and it is worth practising. Some of the methods which can be used are described in the next chapter.

Exercises

1 Lay off a true course from a position 2 miles due south of Royal Sovereign Light to 2 miles south of the red and white buoy in Rye Bay. If the current was setting 080° at 1.4 knots and the vessel's speed was 5 knots what would be the course to steer to counteract the current to make good the course required?

2 Using the same course line from Royal Sovereign to Rye Bay Buoy find the course to steer if the current was setting 280° at 1.8 knots. 5 degrees leeway for a SE wind. Vessel's speed 5 knots.

3 If you left the position off Royal Sovereign at 1000 plot the EP for 1200 if the current was setting 080° at 1.5 knots and the vessel was making 5° leeway from a northerly wind. Vessel's speed estimated at 4.5 knots.

4 From the above question find the new course to steer to make the position off Rye Bay Buoy allowing for current setting as in exercise 3. As the wind has died there is no leeway. Vessel's speed is still 4.5 knots.

11
POSITION FIXING

Sources of Position Lines

The first ingredient in establishing your position is a **position line.** A position line is any bearing of a fixed object which you take from your vessel and plot on the chart. A single position line tells you that your position must be somewhere along that line, but you do not know just where. If you obtain another position line from a different bearing then the point at which the two cross should be the actual position and this is a 'fix'.

Position lines can be obtained from compass bearings of objects which are marked on the chart and can be recognised. It is no use using the bearing of, for instance, a headland of whose identity you are not certain. Charts are not confused with a great deal of land detail, but do show any conspicuous buildings such as churches which might be useful to the navigator. These are often marked with the abbreviation 'conspic'. Navigation buoys do not make good objects for bearings as there is a possibility they may have shifted in bad weather.

Radio bearings can also give position lines using a direction finding set. Many lighthouses are radio beacons transmitting continuous morse signals for this purpose. Their frequencies and identification letters are listed in the nautical almanac. They are often linked in groups so that in any one place a bearing can be taken from more than one, thus enabling you to get a fix on the chart.

In the absence of visual or radio bearings it is possible to obtain a position line from soundings. If you take soundings frequently and compare them with the depths shown on the chart (allowing for the state of tide) in the vicinity of your assumed position you may be able to draw up a position line from them.

A position line can also be obtained from a transit and when this is possible gives the most accurate position line of all. A transit is when two prominent objects in the chart are in line. If you can watch out for this possibility then all you have to do is draw a line through them extending seawards and you will know that as they come into line one behind the other that you have a good position line.

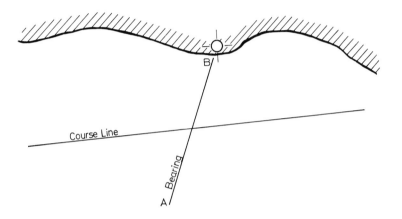

A position line obtained with a single bearing. All that can be said is that the yacht is somewhere along the line AB.

Cross Bearings

This is the simplest and most reliable of all visual methods of obtaining a fix. Two crossed bearings should in theory give you a fix, but due to the difficulty of taking accurate bearings from a small boat it is always better to take three if possible. The result of plotting three bearings hardly ever results in the lines crossing neatly at a single point. More usually they create a small triangle known as a 'cocked hat'. You may assume yourself to be in the cocked hat and mark your fix there, putting the time and a small circle round it (the latter to distinguish it from a DR or EP). To make your fix as accurate as possible try to choose bearings of objects which are not too close together and not at extremely wide angles. If you end up with a very large cocked hat it may be wise to re-work the bearings.

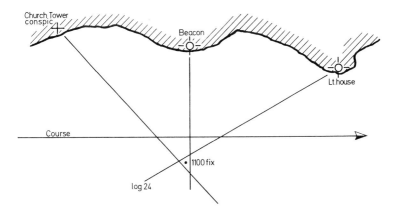

A position fix with three crossed bearings which produce a cocked hat.

The running fix

Frequently it is only possible to see one object to take a bearing and so get a single position line, but by using the vessel's own course and speed it is possible to get a position called a running fix. It has limited accuracy as it depends upon a straight course being steered and an accurate knowledge of the vessel's speed. It must also include allowance for the set of the tide. Nevertheless a running fix is better than nothing if only one object for a bearing is in view. The first example is of a running fix with no current being allowed for.

For this problem assume you are on your course line. Take a bearing of the lighthouse and lay it off on the chart so that it cuts the course line at 1000hrs. After one hour take another bearing of the same lighthouse and lay it off on the chart. Read the log at 1000 and 1100 and lay this distance off along the course line. If it coincides with the 1100 bearing then you are probably on or near the course line, but if it does not then transfer the first bearing (pecked line in diagram) parallel and draw it through the place on the course line where your speed is marked for one hour. Where this first transferred bearing cuts the second bearing is the probable position of the vessel.

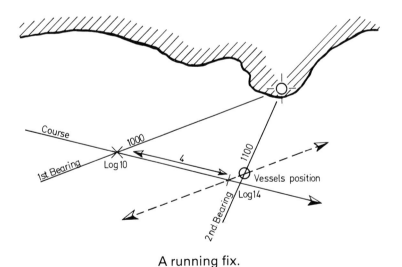

A running fix.

Four Point Bearing

How does this differ to doubling angle on the bow

This is a simple mathematical exercise which uses the fact that in an isoceles triangle the two base angles are equal and the two adjacent sides are equal in length. Single bearings are taken at times which are mathematically suitable.

In the example below, if the course is 270° then to get a four point bearing we need to take the bearing of the lighthouse when it is bearing 45° on the bow ie 315°. To complete the exercise we take another bearing when the lighthouse is abeam (ie at 90° to our course,) in this case when it is bearing 000°. Then the distance run between the bearings will be automatically the distance the vessel is from the lighthouse.

The four point bearing method (four points is the old-fashioned compass equivalent of 45°) used to be a very common way of navigating round a coastline before the use of radar. It can still be very helpful to the yachtsman as a way of altering course round headlands on to the next course.

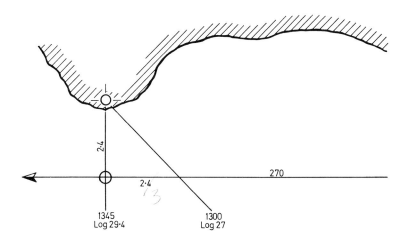

Four point bearing.

Doubling the angle on the bow

Another form of running fix is to take a bearing of an object, say at 25° on the bow, and then a second bearing when the bearing of the same object is 50° on the bow. The distance run on the log between these two bearings will be the distance off the object at the time of the second bearing.

This means again waiting until the bearing is at a certain angle before plotting, but it has the advantage of giving you a distance off the object, which could be useful if there are offlying rocks.

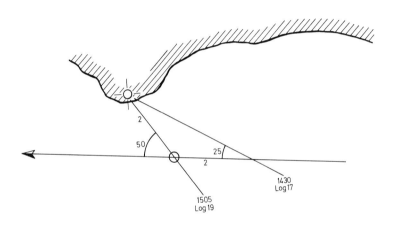

Doubling the angle on the bow.

Running Fix with current

All the above examples can be used when allowing for current. Just plot the rate and direction of the current at the end of the distance run between the bearings and transfer the first bearing parallel through that point at the end of the current, and where the first bearing cuts the second bearing will be the probable position of the vessel.

A is the first bearing, B is the second bearing. The vessel's speed of 5 knots from A to C. Line CD is the set and rate of the current. Pecked line EF is the first bearing transferred to the point D and where it cuts the second bearing B is the vessel's probable position.

A running fix may be combined with a sounding which will give further accuracy of position.

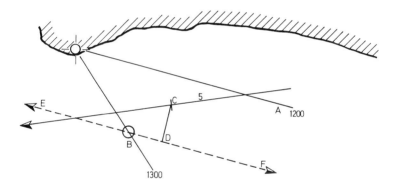

Running fix allowing for current.

Exercises

1 (*Using a running fix*)

A vessel is steering a course of 250° (T) from Dungeness to Beachy Head. At 1130 she takes a bearing of Hastings light bearing 272° (C). An hour later Hastings light is bearing 330° (C). If the vessel's speed is 4 knots what is the vessel's position at 1230? Use variation as 6°W. No deviation.

2 (*Using a running fix*)

A vessel steering 072° (T) takes a bearing of Dungeness Lt which gives 040° (T) and half an hour later takes another bearing which gives 022° (T). If the vessel's speed is 3 knots what is the position of the vessel at the time of the second bearing?

3 (*Using a four point bearing*)

A vessel steering 070° (T) observes Royal Sovereign Light bearing 115° (T) log reads 27. Half an hour later Royal Sovereign Light bore 160° (T). If the vessel's speed was 4 knots what is the distance off Royal Sovereign Light at the time of the second bearing?

4 (*Using a running fix with allowance for current*)

A vessel is steering 008° (T) and observes C. Gris Nez Lt bearing 046° (C). Half an hour later C. Gris Nez Lt bore 085° (C). If the vessel's speed was 5 knots and the current was setting 030° at 1.8 knots what is the vessel's position at the time of the second bearing? Use variation 6°W. No deviation.

5 (*Using cross bearings*)

A vessel steering 045° takes the following bearings at 1200. South Foreland 275° (C), Memorial Beacon 315° (C) and South Goodwin Lt. Vessel 090° (C). What is the vessel's position in latitude and longitude? Variation 6°W. Deviation 2°E.

12
TIDES AND TIDAL STREAMS

The tides are caused by the gravitational pull of the moon and the sun, but mainly by the moon as, although a smaller mass, it is much nearer the earth. The tides therefore follow a lunar cycle. When the moon is in the new and full phases there is a greater rise and fall of tide. These are known as spring tides. When the sun and moon are in opposition and there is a lesser pull on the waters of the earth giving rise to a smaller rise and fall of tide. These are called neap tides and occur at the moon's quarters.

In the waters around the British Isles the tides are mainly semi-diurnal, which means that we have two high tides and two low tides in each 24 hours. The times of high water advance by very roughly an hour each day. This is due to the period of rotation of the earth relative to the moon, or lunar day, which is approximately 24 hours 50 minutes.

The period of approximately 6 hours when the tide is rising is called the **flood** and the time when it is falling is called the **ebb**.

Spring Tides

The period of spring tides occurs twice in the lunar month. The word has nothing to do with the season of the year but comes from an old Norse word signifying 'big'. By looking at the heights given for each day in the tide tables you can see when the spring tides occur and how they build up in height progressively each day, then fall away again as the moon moves to its next phase. At springs the tide will not only reach higher levels, it will also fall lower, leaving a lesser depth of water than at other times. Larger than normal spring tides occur around about the time of the equinoxes in March and September.

Neap Tides

At the two quarters of the moon we have neap tides (from an old word meaning 'nipped', 'cut-off' or 'small'). Then the tides will not reach such high levels, but neither will they fall so low as at other times. The flow is also affected. At periods of neaps the tidal flow in channels and estuaries will be less swift than at springs.

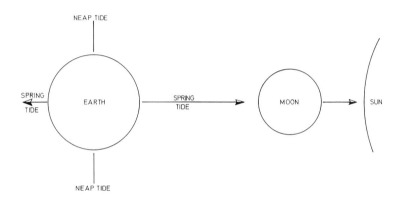

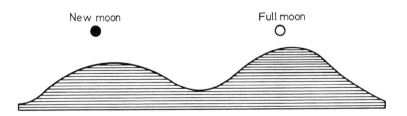

The curve above represents the gradual oscillation of the tides over the cycle of the lunar month. The highest spring range at full moon falls gradually to neaps and rises again to reach a peak at new moon.

Chart Datum

This is the theoretical plane from which the chart makers measure the depths of the sea and mark them on the chart. Chart Datum is set at mean low water ordinary springs (MLWOS) or on more recent charts at the level of lowest astronomical tides (LAT). The latter level allows for any combination of astronomical conditions and is a level reached only very occasionally, usually under storm conditions. Which datum is used is stated on the chart.

Range of Tide

The difference between any high water height and the preceding or succeeding low water height. To find the tidal range at a place for any particular day simply deduct the height shown in the tables for low water from that given for high water.

Mean High Water Springs, etc.

The average level of high water spring tides in any given place. Abbreviated as MWHS. Similarly we have mean low water springs (MLWS), mean high water neaps (MHWN) and mean low water neaps (MLWN).

Mean level

The average height of the tide between high and low waters. It is not the same thing as mean sea level.

Soundings

The name given to the depth of water marked on the chart. This is the depth of water below the level of chart datum and has to be added to any depth given in the tide tables in order to find the amount of water there will actually be there at high water.

Drying Heights

These are heights above chart datum of features such as sandbanks or rock ledges which are periodically covered and uncovered by the tide. They are indicated on charts with a line underneath the figure to distinguish them from other soundings.

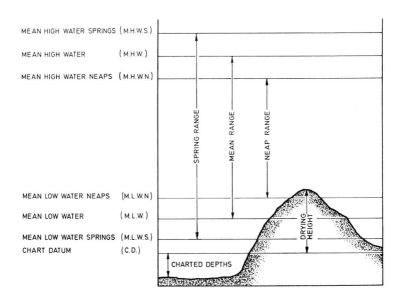

The diagram above illustrates the various terms which are used in connection with the tides.

The Use of Tide Tables

Whenever you are sailing in tidal waters it is important to know the times and heights of high and low water. Annual booklets of local tide tables are published in most yachting ports. Local newspapers also print the information and harbourmasters often arrange for it to be displayed. For a skipper however it is well to be acquainted with the use of the tide tables in the principal nautical almanacs or the Admiralty Tide Tables. For actual use (as opposed to practice) it must be the one for the current year.

These publications give tables for a number of places which are known as **standard ports**, usually the bigger ones used by commercial shipping. As a yachtsman you will often be using smaller places referred to as **secondary ports**. With the information for each standard port the almanacs provide a table of tidal differences for all the secondary ports associated with it, showing by how much you should adjust the times and heights shown for the standard port. For instance, if you were sailing to Ramsgate you would have to use the tide tables for Dover and turning to the adjoining table of tidal differences would find that you have to add 20 minutes from the time of high water and deduct 1.6 metres from the height.

Example Find the times of High and Low water for Dover on 1st May.
Reading from the table the times of high and low water are:
High water 0826 and 2049 with heights of 6.0 and 6.3 metres
Low water 0327 and 1553 with heights of 1.2 and 1.2 metres

To find the times and heights of high and low water at Ramsgate for 2nd August, see the tidal differences on Dover.

Dover High Water	0004	6.6	1224	6.7
Correction for Ramsgate	+ 20	− 1.6	+ 20	− 1.6
Ramsgate High Water	0024	5.0	1244	5.1
Dover Low Water	0759	0.9	2011	0.7
Correction for Ramsgate	− 0 07	− 0.6	−0 07	− 0.6
Ramsgate Low Water	0752	0.3	2004	0.1
	0852	BST	2104	BST

DOVER

HIGH & LOW WATER
1981   G.M.T. ADD 1 HOUR MARCH 22-OCTOBER 25 FOR B.S

MAY				JUNE				JULY				AUGUST			
Time h.min.	Ht. m.	Time h.min.	Ht m.	Time h.min.	Ht. m.	Time h.min.	Ht. m.	Time h.min.	Ht. m.	Time h.min.	Ht. m.	Time h.min.	Ht. m.	Time h.min.	
1 F 0327	1.2	**16** 0447	1.2	**1 M** 0444	0.8	**16** 0518	1.3	**1 W** 0520	0.9	**16** 0530	1.2	**1 Sa** 0713	0.9	**16** 0638	
0826	6.0	0939	5.9	0938	6.5	1024	6.1	1020	6.5	1037	6.2	1144	6.7	1118	
1553	1.2	Sa 1706	1.3	1705	0.9	Tu 1734	1.3	1742	1.0	Th 1754	1.2	1927	0.8	Su 1902	
2049	6.3	2149	6.2	2159	6.7	2237	6.2	2238	6.6	2247	6.2	—	—	2332	
2 Sa 0424	0.8	**17** 0525	1.1	**2 Tu** 0537	0.6	**17** 0554	1.1	**2 Th** 0621	0.8	**17** 0614	1.1	**2 Su** 0004	6.6	**17** 0717	
0912	6.4	1013	6.1	1028	6.6	1101	6.3	1112	6.6	1109	6.3	0759	0.9	1156	
1647	0.9	Su 1740	1.2	Tu 1757	0.7	W 1814	1.1	Th 1839	0.8	F 1836	1.1	Su 1224	6.7	M 1938	
2135	6.6	2226	6.3	2248	6.8	2312	6.3	2330	6.6	2319	6.3	2011	0.7	—	
3 Su 0516	0.6	**18** 0556	1.1	**3** 0629	0.6	**18** 0634	1.0	**3** 0716	0.8	**18** 0655	1.0	**3** 0043	6.5	**18** 0011	
0957	6.6	1048	6.2	1120	6.7	1133	6.3	1200	6.7	1143	6.5	0837	0.9	0749	
1736	0.7	M 1807	1.1	W 1848	0.7	Th 1853	1.0	F 1933	0.7	Sa 1917	1.0	M 1302	6.7	Tu 1235	
2220	6.8	2302	6.4	2339	6.8	2343	6.2	—	—	2354	6.3	2050	0.8	2009	
4 M 0604	0.5	**19** 0624	1.0	**4** 0721	0.6	**19** 0712	1.0	**4** 0019	6.6	**19** 0733	1.0	**4** 0123	6.4	**19** 0055	
1044	6.8	1122	6.3	1212	6.7	1205	6.3	0806	0.8	1218	6.5	0910	1.1	0819	
1821	0.6	Tu 1838	1.0	Th 1938	0.6	F 1931	1.0	Sa 1243	6.6	Su 1954	0.9	Tu 1340	6.6	W 1317	
2306	6.9	2336	6.4	—	—	—	—	2022	0.7	—	—	2124	1.0	2042	

TIDAL DIFFERENCES ON DOVE

PLACE	MHW		MLW		GUIDING DEPTH AT			
	Tm. Diff. h. min.	Ht. Diff. m.	Tm. Diff. h. min.	Ht. Diff. m.	HWS m.	HWN m.	CD m.	POSITION
Hastings	− 0 05	+ 0.6	− 0 30	0.0	9.0	7.3	1.5	Entrance
Rye (Apprs.)	0 00	+ 0.8	—	—	6.2	4.5	− 1.5	Bar near entrance
Dungeness	− 0 15	+ 1.2	− 0 15	+ 0.2	15.3	13.6	7.3	West Road Anche.
Folkestone	− 0 10	+ 0.4	− 0 10	0.0	5.5	3.1	− 1.6	Alongside Sth Quay
Dover	0 00	0.0	0 00	0.0	7.1	5.7	0.4	Entce. Granville Dock
Deal	+ 0 15	− 0.4	+ 0 05	0.0	10.1	9.0	4.0	Pier Head
Richborough	+ 0 15	− 1.0	—	—	2.8	1.7	− 0.9	Chan to
Ramsgate	+ 0 20	− 1.6	− 0 07	− 0.6	5.0	3.9	0.1	Entrance

All tide tables are in Greenwich Mean Time (GMT). During British Summer Time (BST) one hour must be added. They are also based on predictions which can be upset by meteorological conditions so all calculations should allow for a margin of error to ensure there is always sufficient water under your keel.

Finding the Depth of Water

Although the tide tables enable you to work out the depth of water in a particular place at high and low water (by adding the height in the table to the sounding shown on the chart) there will be times when you need to know that depth at times between low and high waters. This may be when you want to leave a harbour which dries out or has a sand bar, or when you want to find an anchorage. One way of doing this is by making use of the **Twelfths Rule**. The Twelfths Rule is based on the fact that over the six hour period of ebb or flood the tide it will rise or fall at the following rate:

1st hour – 1/12th of range
2nd hour – 2/12th of range
3rd hour – 3/12th of range
4th hour – 3/12th of range
5th hour – 2/12th of range
6th hour – 1/12th of range

As we can find the range of the tide from the tables it is then possible to apply the above to calculate a depth for any hour before or after high water. For example, suppose you need to know the height of tide at Dover at 1230 on June 1st. The tide table shows that HW is 1038 BST and the height of the tide 6.5m. The range (difference between HW and LW) is 5.6m. As it is 2 hours after high water then the tide by then will have fallen 1/12th of its range in the first hour and 2/12ths in the second hour, a total of 3/12ths or 1/4 of the range. One quarter of 5.6 = 1.4. Therefore the height at Dover at 1230 will be 6.5m − 1.4m = 5.1m approximately.

There is a simplified version of the Twelfths Rule as follows:
1 hour before or after HW the tide will have risen or fallen 1/12 of the range.
2 hours before or after it will have risen or fallen 1/4 of its range
3 hours before or after it will have risen or fallen 1/2 of its range.

Tidal Curves

It must be emphasised that the Twelfths Rule is only an approximation, but for most of the time for practical purposes will give the yachtsman a good enough estimate of the depth of the water to be found at a particular time. It would be foolish not to allow at least an additional two or three feet under the keel as a safety margin.

The Twelfths Rule assumes that the tide behaves in a symmetrical pattern and behaves in the same way in all places at all times which is not the case. A more accurate way of arriving at the depth is by using the tidal curves published in the Admiralty Tide Tables and in some nautical almanacs. These plot as a graph the rise and fall of the tide for each hour for each standard port, with a different curve for springs and neaps, and can be used to find the height of tide at any particular time.

Tidal Streams

As we have discussed in the chapter on chartwork a knowledge of tidal streams in open water are also essential to the navigator. The main flood stream flows in an easterly direction up the English Channel and simultaneously up the Irish Sea and round the tip of Scotland. This is a horizontal movement of water flowing for approximately six hours in one direction and six hours in the other. These may have a rate of two knots or more which can considerably affect the speed of a sailing yacht. Without an engine it may at times be impossible to make headway against an adverse tidal stream and it may be prudent to anchor until it turns in your favour. Remember that the information you need about tidal streams will be found either from the tidal diamonds on the chart or from a tidal atlas. Most tidal stream information is based on the time of HW Dover, so you need Dover tide tables for reference and these will be in any nautical almanac. However many tidal atlases are based on a standard port in the area they cover.

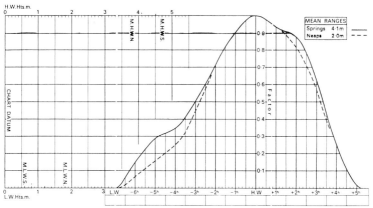

PORTSMOUTH
MEAN SPRING AND NEAP CURVES
Springs occur 2 days after New and Full Moon.

Example of a tidal curve.

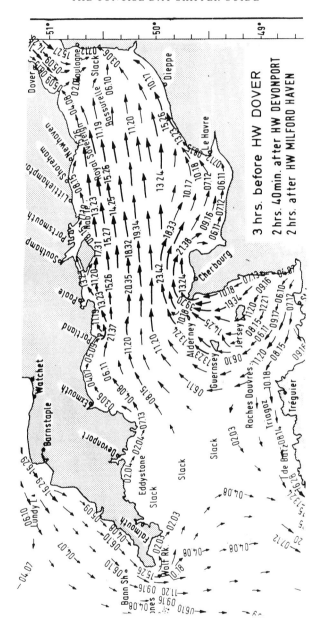

Page from a tidal stream atlas of the English Channel.

Races and Overfalls

Races are areas of turbulent water which occur where a headland sticks out into a fast moving tidal stream. Some are quite extensive and notorious, like the one off Portland Bill in Dorset. Races are marked on the charts and should be avoided by small vessels, especially at springs and when the wind is against the tide, as dangerous, confused seas can be created. Similar conditions are caused by overfalls (also marked on the chart) which occur when the tidal stream flows over an uneven or rocky sea bed.

Tidal streams also often set into a bay, which can mean you find yourself closer inshore than you expected when sailing from one headland to another. A classic cause of sailing ship disasters was being 'embayed' for this reason and not being able to beat out against the wind. So make sure you allow for the set of the tidal streams.

Off Portland Bill the tide may be running at 6 knots. In the Alderney Race in the Channel Islands it reaches 10 knots. The prudent yachtsman will avoid areas like these, but by good passage planning will ensure that he makes the tidal streams work for him. Even going up and down the Solent having worked the tides right can make a world of difference to the day's pleasure.

Exercises

1 Find the times and heights of high water at Dover for 17th June.
2 Find the times and heights of low water at Dover for 18th August.
3 Find the times and heights of high and low water at Hastings on 18th August.
4 Find the times and heights of high and low water at Richborough on the 4th July.
   (Use the tide and difference table reproduced on an earlier page).

13
PILOTAGE

In the context of this chapter pilotage means the safe conduct of a vessel in and out of harbour and in the immediate vicinity of the coastline.

It means first of all that you must become thoroughly acquainted with your home port and all its marks, hazards and safe channels. This may come from sailing as crew with an experienced skipper or getting someone to show you. When you plan to visit other ports you must obtain as much similar knowledge as you can beforehand. This will come from a careful study of the chart and from one of the various yachtsmen's pilot books which have plans, photographs, aerial views, etc of most of the small anchorages and harbours in popular sailing areas. Make a note of all special features of the port, especially buoys and other navigation marks, and any dangers in the approaches.

By this means you will build up a mental picture before you set off. Don't rely on studying the chart as you enter. A harbour or estuary is often well hidden in the coastline until you are almost on top of it and features which may seem obvious can sometimes be difficult to identify. Headlands particularly look very different from different angles and in different lights so the more you study in advance the better.

As you enter a strange harbour:

Remember there is likely to be a lot of other traffic around.
Keep to the starboard side of a narrow channel.
Allow for the effect of strong winds or tides which may set you off course.
On river bends remember that the deep water will be on the outside of the bend.
Give buoys and moored craft plenty of room and watch that the tide does not set you down on them.
Keep a look out astern for overtaking craft.

Transits

Transit bearings are a good way of ensuring that you are avoiding any dangers when you are entering a harbour or anchorage. If possible choose objects which can be seen in line ahead or astern and then sail down this line of transit. The diagram shows how easy it is to clear a danger with transit bearings. Sometimes harbour plans show transit bearings already for you to use. These are known as **leading marks**. These marks are then joined by a line on the chart known as the **leading line**. The marks which are used are often beacons and lights, erected for the purpose, but other conspicuous objects such as church towers are used as well. At night some leading marks are lit, making it easier to enter safely in the dark, but this is rare in smaller harbours and anchorages. When you find two objects in transit you should take a bearing of them with the compass and compare the bearing with that on the chart. This will ensure that you have the correct objects and will, if you have time, give you a compass check at the same time. It is not easy keeping leading marks in transit. One will frequently open out against the other and course will have to be altered to keep the vessel on the transit.

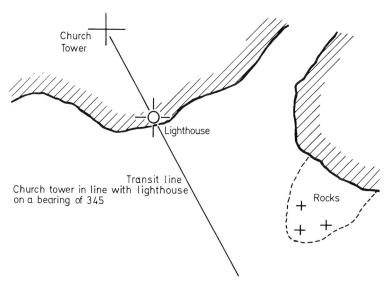

Church tower in line with lighthouse
on a bearing of 345

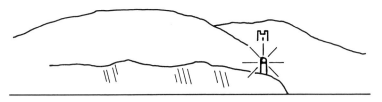

Church and lighthouse in transit

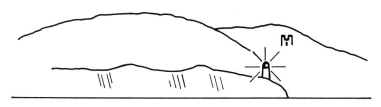

Church open to right of lighthouse

Clearing Bearings

This is similar to using a transit but relies on a compass bearing of a single identified object to give a safe line of entry clearing all dangers. Sometimes two are useful as in the example shown. In this case any course between 005 and 030 will take the craft into harbour clear of the two groups of outlying rocks. The two lines are especially useful for a yacht working to windward as she could tack between those two limits – on starboard tack until the hotel bears 030 and then on port tack until the hotel bears 005.

Clearing lines will be found already printed on some charts, with the bearing shown alongside, but make a habit of finding your own and drawing them in.

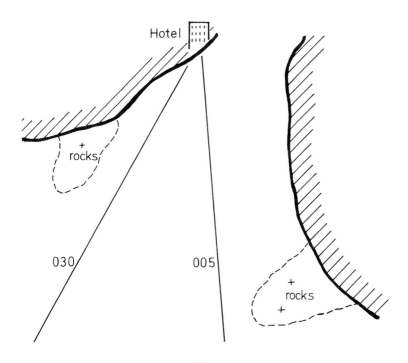

Buoyage

Buoys are used to mark a safe channel through a harbour or estuary or to show a safe course round some danger. It is essential to know the system. They are distinguished by colour and shape and at night by lights. Since 1977 a common system known as the IALA buoyage system has been in use in European waters. There are five types described below.

Lateral buoys. These mark the port and starboard sides of a deep water channel. Port hand buoys are red and can shaped. Starboard hand buoys are green and conical. If lit they have red and green lights respectively. Sometimes they are fitted with a topmark to make them clearer. This will be can shaped on a port buoy and a cone or triangle on a starboard.

Lateral buoys mark the channel according to the direction of the main flood tide, that is from seaward. You will leave starboard hand buoys on your starboard side and port hand buoys to your port, but you must remember this is reversed when you are sailing in the other direction. It is also needful to remember that if you pick up a lateral buoy at sea it will be marking a channel in accordance with conventional buoyage direction. In the example below the lateral buoys are marking the channels in an easterly and northerly direction so if you were sailing west or south you would have to use them in the reverse (ie leaving starboard hand buoys to port and vice versa).

It is always prudent to follow the buoyed channels unless you have thorough local knowledge. However they are laid out for larger vessels and yachts can usually with safety sail just on the wrong side of the buoys. If there is a lot of commercial traffic this is often the most comfortable position.

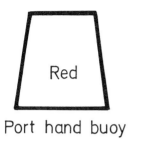

Port hand buoy

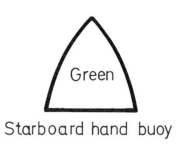

Starboard hand buoy

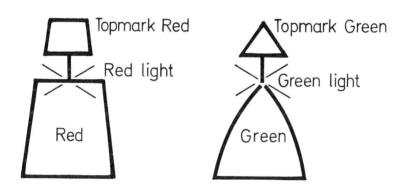

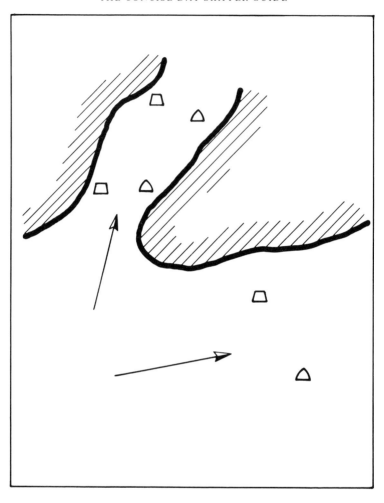

Lateral buoyage on the left into a harbour, and on the right in the open sea following the conventional direction of tide.

Conventional direction of lateral buoyage round the British Isles. It is mainly the direction of the main flood tide, but not in all places.

Cardinal Buoys. These buoys mark shoals or dangers and indicate where the mariner will find safe navigable water. They are called cardinal because they mark the four cardinal points of the compass – north, south, east and west. In practice they mark the quadrants from north west to north east, north east to south east, south east to south west and south west to north west. The buoys are placed according to the side of the danger or hazard they mark, so that the north end of a group of rocks is marked by a north cardinal buoy, telling the mariner to pass north of that buoy to clear the danger. Similarly a west cardinal buoy marks the western edge of a hazard, an east cardinal buoy marks the eastern side and a south cardinal buoy the south side. To identify it each buoy has a different top mark, colour and light.

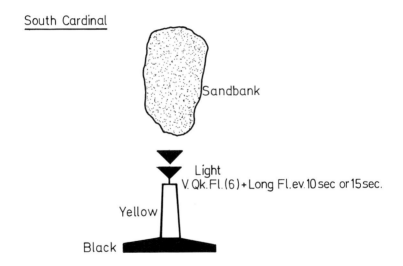

South Cardinal

Sandbank

Light
V. Qk. Fl. (6) + Long Fl. ev. 10 sec. or 15 sec.

Yellow

Black

North Cardinal

Light
V. Qk. Fl. White

Black

Yellow

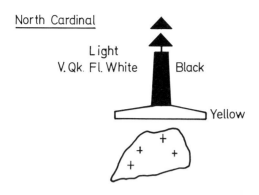

East Cardinal

(Egg shaped for east)

Light
V. Qk. Fl. (3) ev. 10 sec.

Black

Yellow

Black

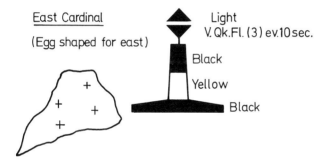

West Cardinal

Light
V. Qk. Fl. (9) ev. 10 secs or 15 sec.

Yellow

Black

Yellow

Sandbank

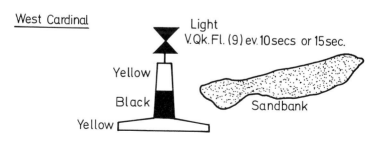

113

Isolated Danger Mark A buoy will be placed over a danger which is isolated, but which has navigable water all round it. An example might be a wreck which has sunk in deep water, but the mast near the surface. The shape is the same as the cardinal buoy, ie pillar or spar, but the colours are black and red, and the topmarks are two black spheres above each other. The light when fitted would be white Gp. F1 (2) – Group flashing two flashes.

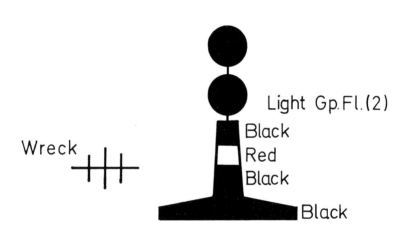

Safe Water Marks. Sometimes placed where there is navigable water all round, such as to mark the middle of a wide channel where the lateral buoys may not be in sight. They may also be used as 'landfall' buoys, marking the start of a lateral buoyage channel at the seaward end.

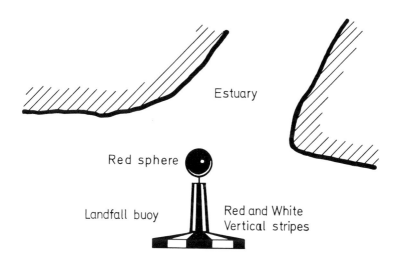

Estuary

Red sphere

Landfall buoy

Red and White
Vertical stripes

The light when fitted is white, isophase, occulting or one long flash every 10 seconds

Special Marks. Not meant for navigation. They are cautionary and mark such things as a military exercise zone, pipeline or cable, recreation area, etc. They are sometimes used to mark a new danger not yet charted, such as a recent wreck or newly discovered sandbank. Special mark buoys are yellow with a yellow cross topmark and if lit will have a yellow light.

Buoys and Navigation

Buoys are an aid to navigation. Never attempt to moor or tie up to one. Identify each one as it comes into sight as a check on your position and note in the log what time you pass it. Many of them have distinctive names painted on their sides which helps you to be certain. Some authorities caution against relying on buoys for position fixing as they may have dragged in bad weather or temporarily taken off station, but this is not very common.

Questions

1 What is a transit bearing?
2 What is a clearing bearing?
3 Name some precautions to be taken when navigating in restricted waters.
4 You are leaving an estuary and see a red can shaped buoy. Which side shall you leave it.
5 A cardinal buoy with a topmark of two upward pointing cones has to be passed on which side?

14

VISUAL AIDS TO NAVIGATION

Lighthouses have been placed where they are to give warning of dangers such as protruding headlands or reefs of rock. Where the danger is a shifting sandbank where no light tower could be built lightships are used. Some of the latter are now being replaced by Lanbys (large automatic navigational buoys). Light beacons are more commonly used to light the safe entrance to a harbour or estuary.

Such marks as these are valuable to the navigator by day as well as by night. They are usually of distinctive shape so providing an easily identifiable object for a position check. They are in many cases also the source of radio navigation signals and of sound signals during fog. They may also house watchful eyes able to give warning to craft in danger or alert rescue services, though an increasing number are nowadays automated and unmanned.

Lighthouse information

Admiralty charts give a good deal of information about lighthouses all of which may be useful at different times. Every lighthouse is marked by a star and the precise position is indicated by a circle inside the star. Lightships are shown with a small boat shape with the circle at the bottom of the hull. In addition the following information is usually given:

The characteristic of the light
Range of the light
Its colour or colours
The height of the tower
Sound signals used in fog
Radio identification signals

This information is also listed in *Reed's Nautical Almanac* together with the position of the light by latitude and longitude. Many pilot books and other publications for the cruising yachtsman also contain photographs or drawings of lighthouse towers to aid identification. Many are distinctively painted (e.g. with red and white bands) to make them conspicuous. This also applies to the less frequently encountered structures known as daymarks. These are unlit and unmanned and there simply to provide the mariner with a position check. When planning a passage it is good practice to list all the lighthouse likely to be encountered, together with their features and characteristics, so you know what to look out for.

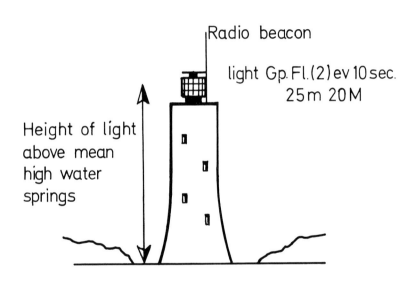

Light characteristics

To make it possible for seamen to know which light they are observing at night each one displays its lights in a different manner and this pattern is known as the light characteristic. This is printed on the chart in abbreviated form. There are endless permutations. Examples of the main types are given below. There is a full listing in 'Symbols and Abbreviations Used On Admiralty Charts' (Chart no. 5011). The letters in brackets are the new international abbreviations which are gradually replacing the older ones on the charts.

Gp F12 10 sec. (F12) A group flashing light. It will flash in groups at intervals, in this case 2 flashes with an interval of 10 seconds between groups.

Occ (Oc) Occulting. A steady light with a short period of dark at regular intervals.

Gp Occ 2 (Oc2) Group occulting. When there is a group of dark periods (in this example 2) at regular intervals.

Iso Isophase. Light and dark periods of equal length.

Qk Fl (Q) Quick flashing. A continuous rapid flash

Qk F12 (Q2) Group quick flashing. A group of rapid flashes (in this case 2) followed by a period of dark.

Alt WR (Al WR) Alternating. A light which flashes with alternate colours, in this case white and red.

F Fixed. A steady light. It may be white or coloured as the chart will show.

The Characteristic of the Light

Gp. Fl
(Fl. 2)

This means group flashing i. e. The light will flash
in groups of, say, 2 flashes every 10 seconds

Occ.
(Oc.)

This is a steady light with a short period
of dark before the next steady light

Gp. Occ.(2)

This is two or more steady periods of light in a group
with short periods of dark regularly repeated

Iso.

This is where the light and dark periods are
of equal length

Qk. Fl.
(Q)

A continuous quick flash which is regularly repeated

Qk. Fl(2)
(Q.(2))

A group of quick flashes, in this case groups of
two quick flashes regularly repeated

Alt. WR.
(Al. WR.)

This is a light which alternates in colour
in successive flashes

120

Range and Height of Lights

How far away can a light be seen? This depends on which of three definitions is being used.

Luminous range is the distance depending only on the intensity of the light and the meteorological conditions at the time. **Nominal range** is that given by the intensity of the light when the meteorological visibility is at least 10 sea miles. This is the one which is usually given on the modern charts. **Geographical range** is the maximum distance a light can theoretically be seen allowing for the height of the tower, the height of the observer's eye above sea level and the curvature of the earth. This fact can be used to work out how far away the vessel is from a light when it is first spotted. On a long night passage you may want to work out the geographical distance in order to estimate what time you might expect to pick up a light. There are tables in the nautical almanac enabling you to do this, known as 'The table of rising or dipping lights'. All you need to use them is the height of the lighthouse tower from the chart and an estimate of your own eye level above the sea.

Lighthouse heights are always given in metres above MHWS. Allowance should be made for the height of tide if it has a very low elevation above sea level. The height can also be used by the navigator in daylight. When a position line has been obtained from a bearing of the light the angle between the boat and the lantern tower can be measured with a sextant. Tables of sextant angles in the nautical almanac will then tell you how far away from the light you are and if this is measured off on the position line you have an excellent fix.

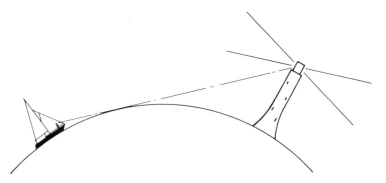

Geographical range of a lighthouse.

Sectored lights

Most lighthouses display a white light in accordance with their particular characteristic but as we saw above some alternate with a coloured light. There are however others which show a white light in one direction and one or more colours in another direction. These are known as sectored lights. The coloured sector is often used to signify an area of danger lying to the side of the lighthouse on which that sector of light is visible. Portland Bill light for instance shows a white light GpFl(4) 20 secs with a fixed red light over the Shambles Shoals. The Needles light has red, white and green sectors. The red light is visible over the Shingles Bank and the green between the shore and a group of offshore rocks.

To sail from a white into a coloured sector should alert the skipper to the fact that he has probably gone off course. The sectored lights can have a positive value as well. The chart will often show the bearings between which the different sectors are visible. If you are at the point where you are leaving one sector and the other is just becoming visible you can use this bearing for a position line.

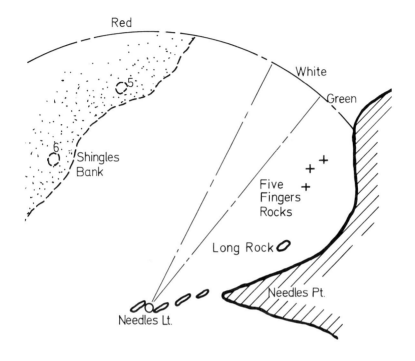

Sectored light showing white over safe water,
red and green in the direction of danger areas.

Sound Signals

Some lighthouses are equipped with fog signals. Like the lights they are different from each other and will be described on the chart or in the nautical almanac. Sound signals are much less reliable than lights. It is often difficult to tell just what direction the sound is coming from. The distance over which they can be heard varies greatly with atmospheric conditions and there can be areas, often quite close to the station, where they are inaudible. It may also happen that you are sailing in thick fog and hear no warning signal because a station only a short distance away is standing in brilliant sunshine.

The different types of fog signal with the appropriate chart description are:

Dia (Diaphone). Works on compressed air and emits a powerful low pitched sound ending with a noticeable grunt.
Horn Some give a powerful steady note while others make sounds of varying pitch
Siren Many different types which vary in sound and power
Reed A weak high pitched sound

Radio Signals

Lighthouses fitted with radio beacons (automatic transmissions from which bearings can be taken with direction finding receivers) are marked RoBn on the chart. Each has a distinctive call sign which is usually two letters in Morse. PB for instance identifies Portland Bill. The frequency and timing of transmissions and the signals are listed in nautical almanacs. These radio beacons are in a linked system so that several may be taken at the same time from the same position to give a fix.

Many are also equipped with Racon (RC on the chart). This is a radar responder beacon which gives off a signal when triggered by a vessel's radar set.

Questions

1 On a chart what information would you find about a lighthouse?
2 What does the following mean: Gp Fl (3) ev.15 40 m 27M &
   F.R.G. 37m 11 M?
3 What is an occulting light?
4 How do charts express the height of a lighthouse?
5 Fog signals should be treated with caution. Why?

15

PASSAGE PLANNING

Taking a small boat to sea is always an adventure. Never let the excitement of it prevent you from careful thought about what you are doing. However small your craft you, as skipper, are responsible for the safety of all on board. Never underestimate the sea and never make any trip without proper forethought. To make a safe passage anywhere, even to the next harbour down the coast, needs planning. Let us look at the factors which must come into your passage plan.

Distance

Is the proposed passage feasible? Measure the distance and decide whether you have a reasonable chance of reaching your destination in the time available. Might it be too long for the endurance of your crew, or their level of enthusiasm? Don't overestimate the distance that can be covered by a sailing boat. The wind strength may be variable and with headwinds you might have to sail double the straight line distance. A power boat can make a more certain estimate of arrival time.

Chartwork

Get out your charts well in advance and lay off the course lines you need to sail to reach your destination. Write the compass course and distance for each leg of the passage. It is also a good idea to mark in the likely DR position at hourly intervals and work out your ETA (Expected Time of Arrival). At the same time make a note of the navigational aids you will pass (lighthouses, buoys, etc) and the principal coastal features such as headlands. Read what the pilot

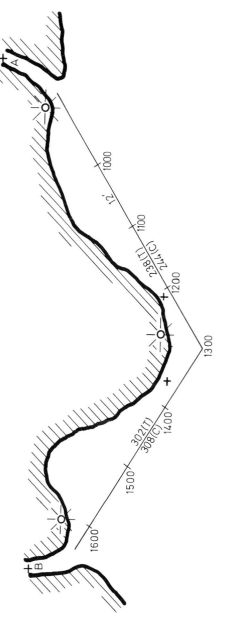

How courses can be plotted in advance when passage planning. Some factors like wind force and direction and leeway
will not be known so different course will probably have to be
sailed, but you will know what course and speed you need to
make good to achieve your objective and be able to make
decisions accordingly.

127

books say about the area. Memorise all principal features and keep a note of them in a plastic wallet handy on board so it can be quickly referred to.

Close study of the chart in advance cannot be stressed too strongly. Your planned course line will of course be laid to take you clear of all dangers, but make sure they do so with a good margin. Leeway, tidal set, arithmetical errors in navigation, inattentive steering are all factors which can combine to put you much closer to them than you think.

Tides

Tidal calculations can all be made in advance as part of your passage planning. You will want to know first if there is enough water for leaving harbour and if you are some way up an estuary you may want to leave on the ebb. However, it is no use leaving immediately after HW only to find that you are spending the next two hours out at sea punching against an adverse tidal stream and getting nowhere. Advance working out of the tides may show that by delaying your departure for an hour or two you could pick up a favourable stream and have a much more pleasant and satisfying day. You will also want to know what the tide will be doing at the destination port at your ETA. Don't regard the tides as an enemy. Learn to work them to your advantage as seamen have done for centuries.

Weather

Planning for the weather can only be done in the final stages, but you could be taking an interest in forecasts for a few days in advance to see how the general situation is developing. Before you sail you will want the latest forecasts (see next chapter on meteorology) to see how they affect your passage plan and your ETA. In the face of a very bad forecast you will not of course go at all, but even when it is reasonably good you should be prepared for the forecast being wrong and have contingency plans. As part of your passage planning you should note what shelter and harbours of refuge there may be en route to your destination in case you need to use them in worsening weather. Check them in the pilot books and see how safe they are to enter. Entry to some harbours is not advised if they are on a lee shore in strong winds or at certain states of the tide. Of course the reason for wanting an alternative anchorage may not be as dramatic as that, but simply that the wind fell light and you didn't get as far as you had hoped.

Boat Readiness

Compile a check list of essentials to be used before every passage. It will include the following.

All safety equipment on board and properly stowed
Adequate fuel supply
Food and water – enough for having to stay at sea longer than you intended
Batteries fully charged up
Engine starting without trouble
Navigation lights working

Crew Readiness

Before you sail brief the crew. Even if it is just the family it pays to be methodical about it. Tell them the salient points of your passage plan. See that they all know where safety equipment is stowed and how it works. Make sure they know what jobs they are to do and are confident about them. If in doubt have a run through before you go. It is so much easier to coach them in harbour than at sea. Finally make sure they are all feeling fit and up to the voyage ahead.

Notifying Your Plans

It is wise to let someone ashore know what your plans are, where you intend to sail and when you expect to arrive. It is equally important to phone them when you have arrived so they can stop worrying. The coastguard service runs a scheme which small boat skippers should take advantage of. You fill in a card with the name and telephone number of your shore contact, your planned destination and ETA and a description of your yacht. Then if you are seriously overdue the rescue services have something to go on and that much more chance of finding you.

The Log Book

On passage you should keep a log book. You can buy one or simply rule up an old exercise book. In it you should record at hourly intervals the distance covered according to the log (hence 'log book'), course being steered, wind strength and direction and barometer readings. You should also note the time of departure and landfall, change of course and of passing any navigation marks and when you stop and start the engine. When a new object comes into view note its bearing and the time in the log.

Apart from forming a pleasant record for the skipper (you can enter the names of the crew for the occasion, decorate it with photographs, etc), the log book has two practical functions. If you become lost or uncertain of your position you can use the information you have recorded to work back your navigational reckoning and check it. A log is also accepted as an official record and can, if duly signed and witnessed, be produced in evidence in a court of law. It could therefore be useful if you were party to a collision or other incident.

Questions

1 List some entries which should be made in a deck log
2 What publications might you take with you on a coastal passage?
3 How could the coastguard help you?
4 What does ETA mean?

16
NAVIGATION IN RESTRICTED VISIBILITY

Taking a small boat to sea in fog is a definite hazard to be avoided if possible. Never set out when there is fog about or forecast. It is not the only form of restricted visibility to beware of. An approaching depression bringing rain and drizzle can often reduce visibility to danger level. Heat haze produces similar difficulties.

Of course it is not always possible to avoid sailing in poor visibility as it can come down suddenly and without warning. The coasts of the British Isles are prone to these conditions so it is important that skippers should have a good knowledge of the precautions to be taken. In the North Sea the number of days in the year with good visibility is no more than one in three. It is always worth remembering that even in clear conditions the visible horizon from the deck of the average yacht, with the eye level only a few feet above the sea, is restricted to about three miles.

Precautions if Caught in Fog

Position. As soon as you see that fog is likely to envelop you try to obtain a fix of your position before all objects which might be useful for bearings are obliterated. If you have a radio direction finding set or electronic instruments for giving your position use them and plot on the chart. If you are relying on visual fixes plot a regular DR and EP once the fog has come down.

Look-Out In fog don't just leave look-out to the person at the helm. Put somebody else on the job as well. On larger yachts post one up forward. Cut down talking and any other unnecessary noise. You will be relying on your ears as much as your eyes and it doesn't help if everybody is chattering.

Radar If your radar reflector wasn't already in position then hoist it now. If you possess a radar set use it to spot other vessels, but remember it is in addition to, and not in place of, visual look out. With caution you may be able to safely enter harbour on your radar.

Safety. The biggest danger in fog is of course collision and consequent sinking. Have everybody in lifejackets at the onset of fog. If anybody went overboard in fog it would be impossible to find them so safety harnesses should be the rule for everybody on deck.

Sound Signals. Sound your foghorn or make an alternative sound signal according to the Collision Regulations at least every two minutes and listen carefully for the signals of other craft. If you hear another signal which seems to be forward of your beam then take the way off your vessel until you can work out what the other is doing. Remember that it is unlikely that your sound signal will be heard from the bridge of a large ship and it is far from certain that you will have been picked up on radar.

Speed. If you are under power it would be wise to reduce speed at the onset of fog. Under sail it is unlikely that you will be going fast enough to reduce speed.

Seeking Safety. If you are not far from port and feel confident enough of your position when you have taken a fix, then it may be safe to put back in, provided the entrance is not a difficult one. Alternatively look on the chart for a safe place to anchor until the weather clears. If the shoreline has no off-laying rocks it is a useful dodge to sail into it slowly at right angles, checking the soundings as you go. When you are in about 5 metres of water you can anchor until the fog clears. Anchored in shallow water you have the comfort of knowing that there will be no large craft moving about and likely to crash into you. On no account anchor in a narrow channel. If you have to remain at sea shape a course that keeps you out of shipping lanes.

Fog Signals

A power driven vessel under way (which might mean anything from a motor boat to a supertanker), sounds 1 prolonged blast every 2 minutes.

A power driven under way but stopped and not making way through the water, sounds 2 prolonged blasts every 2 minutes.

A variety of vessels sound 1 long blast followed by 2 short blasts when under way in fog. They include vessels not under command (ie out of control), restricted in their ability to manoeuvre, constrained by their draught, fishing vessels, towing vessels and sailing vessels.

Ships at anchor or aground are expected to make their position known by the rapid ringing of a bell for 5 seconds every minute.

None of these sound signals is obligatory for craft of less than 12 metres length, but they are instead required to use any means to make an efficient sound signal at intervals of not more than two minutes.

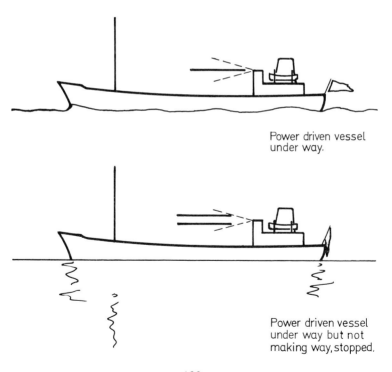

Power driven vessel under way.

Power driven vessel under way but not making way, stopped.

Questions

1 What is a radar reflector used for?
2 How can you find out where you are in fog?
3 What is the sound signal for a sailing vessel in fog?
4 If you heard a prolonged blast in fog what sort of vessel would this be?
5 List some of the precautions you would take on the approach of fog.

17
METEOROLOGY

The weather is probably the most important factor which determines whether you set sail or not. For several days before an intended passage you should have been looking at the weather charts on television or in the newspapers and gaining an idea of the general pattern of the weather. Immediately prior to departure you will need more precise information for the areas you are going.

Sources of Weather Information

Shipping Forecasts These are broadcast on Radio 4 four times a day, every day including Sunday. They are at 0033, 0555, 1355 and 1750 local time (ie they don't alter with the clocks going on for summer time). They follow a set pattern consisting of the following. **General Synopsis** which describes the general pattern of highs and lows with their position and direction. **Forecast** for each of the sea areas for the next 24 hours including wind strength and direction and visibility. **Reports** from coastal stations. Not a forecast but a report of actual conditions (wind speed and direction, visibility, barometer, etc) a few hours before the broadcast.

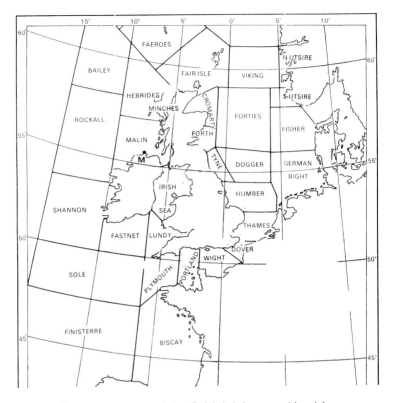

Sea areas around the British Isles used in shipping forecasts.

Inshore Waters Forecasts For the day skipper planning a short coastal passage these will often be more relevant than the main shipping forecast. They cover conditions up to 12 miles offshore. Broadcasts are at 0038 on Radio 4 and 0655 on Radio 3 every day. There may be some regional variations with the timing of these forecasts and they should be checked in the *Radio Times*.

Local Radio Most local radio stations in coastal areas have regular forecasts geared to yachtsmen and conditions in inshore waters. Some nautical almanacs list them, but if not a phone call to the local office will soon elicit the times and wavelengths.

Marinecall This is a British Telecom recorded information service for each of 15 different coastal areas covering the whole coastline. Forecasts are up-dated twice every 24 hours, more frequently for the English Channel in summer. There is a different telephone number for each area, but the charge is the same no matter where you are calling from. There is an equivalent land forecast called Weatherline.

Meteorological Office Anybody may call the Met. Office for a forecast and there are 16 local weather centres throughout the country – Bristol, Birmingham, Cardiff, Leeds, London, Manchester, Newcastle, Norwich, Nottingham, Plymouth, Southampton, Aberdeen, Glasgow, Orkney, Shetland and Belfast.

Other Sources Harbour masters, marinas and yacht clubs will often post up the forecast for the local area at some convenient point

Terms Used in Weather Forecasts

Gale Warnings Gale warnings are issued when the wind is expected to reach Force 8 or more (see section on Beaufort Scale below). They precede all other information in the BBC shipping forecasts and are additionally broadcast at convenient breaks in programmes. Gales are described as being 'soon' (within the next 6 hours), 'imminent' (in the next 12 hours) or 'forecast' (in the next 24 hours).

It is important to remember that these forecasts are geared to commercial shipping. A wind of force 6 is sometimes called 'a yachtsman's gale'. In a small boat with wind over tide and a young family crew force 4 can be enough of a handful. It is not just the wind force which is a criterion of danger. You must take all the other factors into consideration as well.

Until fairly recently visual gale warnings used to be hoisted at coastguard stations, but this is no longer done. An upward pointing black cone indicated a gale from a northerly direction, a downward pointing one a southerly gale. The practice is carried on by some yacht clubs, marinas and harbour masters, or there may be some other form of local signal to look out for.

Isobars These are the lines you see on a weather map and they are joining up places of equal barometric pressure. The closer the lines the stronger will be the wind. You can also learn to tell the wind direction from them. In a High the wind will be roughly in the same direction as the isobars in a clockwise direction. In a Low they will follow the isobars anti-clockwise, but not so closely as in a high. The winds are drawn more into the centre of the depression making an angle with the isobars.

High Pressure Areas Sometimes called 'anti-cyclones,' or just 'highs.' Caused when the wind (in the northern hemisphere) blows anti-clockwise around a centre of high pressure. In summer they produce settled spells of fine weather because they are slow moving

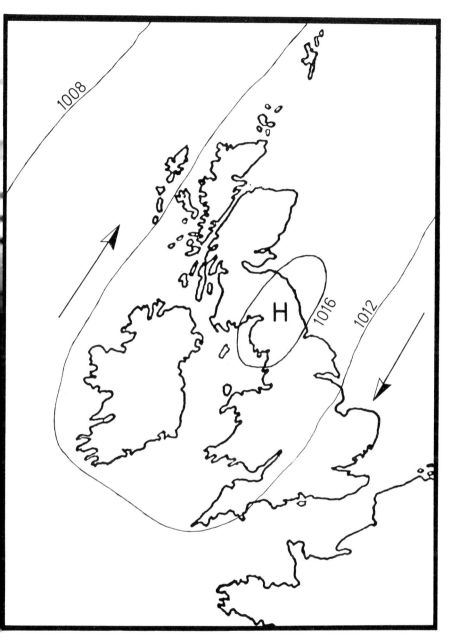

In a high pressure system winds follow the isobars in a clockwise direction.

and will often cause depressions to move away north or south of the British Isles. A disadvantage of high pressure areas is sea haze with poor visibility. There will also be light winds, indicated by the isobars being far apart. In winter high pressure brings clear skies and dry but very cold weather.

Forecasts sometimes refer to a 'ridge of high pressure'. This is a small high pressure zone sandwiched between two lows and gives fine weather for a shorter period of time.

Low Pressure Areas Often called 'depressions' or just 'lows'. They are more complex, forming far away on the other side of the Atlantic. Sometimes they are the remains of tropical storms, but more often form in northern latitudes where cold polar air meets warm tropical air causing a kink at the boundary which develops into a circular movement of air around a low pressure centre. These systems move quickly east at average speeds of 20 to 25 knots, often crossing the British Isles and ending up over Scandinavia where they 'occlude' or 'fill' and effectively fizzle out.

Low pressure systems are characterised by closer isobars. The lower the pressure at the centre the closer they will be and the stronger the winds blowing anti-clockwise around the centre. Gale and storm force winds occur when the pressures are very low. Depressions also bring rain, cloud, mist or fog and generally un-settled conditions.

Typical weather chart showing winds blowing anti-clockwise round the centre of a low press-ure area. Warm front is indicated by the rounded bumps, cold front by the sharp points.

Fronts Lows have two areas called fronts, a cold front and a warm front. They are marked on weather maps as lines running from the centre to the edge. The warm front comes first, marked by little rounded bumps on the chart and is followed after an interval by the cold front, marked by little sharp points. There is a definite sequence associated with the passage of a depression as seen in the diagram. Cirrus clouds will often herald its approach, then the cloud level becomes lower and eventually covers the whole sky. Rain will often come in ahead of the warm front, giving way to persistent drizzle until the arrival of the cold front, following which there may be clearer weather with showers.

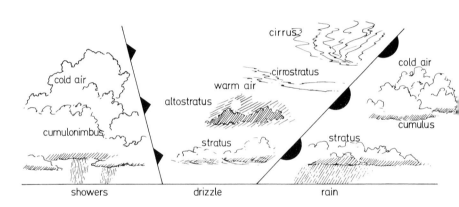

Common weather pattern associated with a depression.

Beaufort Scale

Wind strengths are classified according to the Beaufort Scale, named after the Hydrographer to the Navy who invented it. It is essential for all skippers to be familiar with it and to be able to make their own assessment of the wind force.

Visibility Scale

There is also a scale for visibility, so you may know just what to expect when visibility is mentioned in the shipping forecasts.

Good = more than 5 nautical miles
Moderate = 2 to 5 nautical miles
Poor = 1,000 metres to 2 nautical miles
Fog = below 1,000 metres

No.m.p.h. Name   Conditions

No.	m.p.h.	Name	Conditions
0	Less than 1	Calm	Sea like a mirror
1	1–3	Light air	Ripples with the appearance of scales are formed but without foam crests.
2	4–6	Light breeze	Small wavelets, still short but more pronounced. Crests have a glassy appearance and do not break.
3	7–10	Gentle breeze	Large wavelets. Crests begin to break. Foam of glassy appearance. Perhaps scattered white horses.
4	11–16	Moderate breeze	Small waves, becoming longer: fairly frequent horses.
5	17–21	Fresh breeze	Moderate waves, taking a more pronounced long form; many white horses are formed (chance of some spray).
6	22–27	Strong breeze	Large waves begin to form; the white foam crests are more extensive everywhere (probably some spray).
7	28–33	Near gale	Sea heaps up and white foam from breaking waves begins to be blown in streaks along the direction of the wind.
8	34–40	Gale	Moderately high waves of greater length; edges of crests begin to break into spindrift. The foam is blown in well-marked streaks along the direction of the wind.
9	41–47	Strong gale	High waves. Dense streaks of foam along the direction of the wind. Crests of waves begin to topple, tumble and roll over. Spray may effect visibility.
10	48–55	Storm	Very high waves with long overhanging crests. The resulting foam in great patches is blown in dense white streaks along the direction of the wind. On the whole the surface of the sea takes a white appearance. The tumbling of the sea becomes heavy and shocklike. Visibility affected.
11	56–63	Violent storm	Exceptionally high waves. (Small and medium-sized ships might be for a time lost to view behind the waves). The sea is completely covered with long white patches of foam lying along the direction of the wind. Everywhere the edges of the wave crests are blown into froth. Visibility affected.
12	64+	Hurri-cane	The air is filled with foam and spray. Sea completely white with driving spray; visibility very seriously affected.

Local Winds

Local winds can alter or over-ride the main wind system of the forecast. A land breeze (blowing off the shore) is caused by air that has been cooled overnight and then pushed out to sea by the contours of the land. They are common at the mouths of rivers, but die away as the land warms up during the morning. A sea breeze (blowing on shore) is caused by the land heating up during the day which causes the air to rise and allows an indraught of cooler air from the sea. On warm, sunny days these winds can become quite strong, especially in the afternoons. The effect of local winds will be felt some miles out to sea. Local winds stronger than those forecast may also be caused by the contours of the land, particularly in hilly areas.

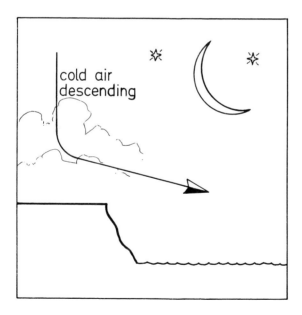

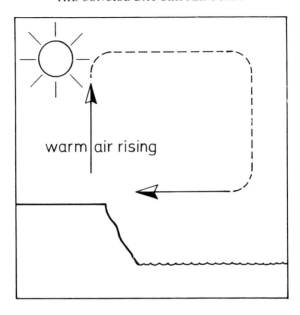

Questions

1 What is the Beaufort Scale?
2 When are the main shipping forecasts broadcast?
3 What causes a sea breeze?
4 What sort of weather do you associate with a depression?
5 When are gale warnings given?

146

ADDITIONAL EXERCISES

1 Find the compass course to steer from a position 2 miles West of C. Gris Nez Lt to Boulogne North Breakwater. Use variation 6W deviation 1E. Find also the distance.

2 Find the compass course to steer from a position 1 mile east of Outer Ruytingen SW buoy to Calais Breakwater allowing for a current setting 030 at 1.3 knots. 5 degrees leeway to be allowed for a force 4 SW wind. Use variation 6W deviation 2W. Vessel's speed 4 knots.

3 Plot the vessel's position from the following bearings:
Royal Sovereign Light Vessel 165 (C)
Beachy Head Lt. House 258 (C)
Use variation 6 W deviation 1W

4 At 1100 BST in Pevensey Bay a vessel is steering 065 (C) and observes a yellow buoy bearing 020 (C) log 15. One hour later the buoy bore 305 (C) log 17.5. If the tide was estimated to be setting 226 at 0.7 knots plot the position of the vessel. A sounding gave 11 metres. Variation 6W.

5 Plot safe courses from a position 0.5 miles north of Dunkerque Light Vessel to Boulogne north breakwater. Pass 1 mile off C. Griz Nez. What is the total distance? What is the ETA at Boulogne if the vessel was at the light vessel at 0900 BST and the speed was estimated at 5 knots. Allow for a tide setting 225 at 0.7 knots for the first two hours and then setting 030 at 1.2 knots for the rest of the passage.

6 Find the height of the tide at Portsmouth at 1200 BST on the 1st June.

7 A vessel steering 265 (C) observes Beachy Head Lt house bearing 310 (C) log 15. When the log read 18 Beachy Head Lt. House bore 355 (C) What is the distance off Beachy Head at the time of the second bearing. Allow 6W variation. No deviation.

8 Give the latitude and longitude of the following:
Varne Light Vessel
Buoy ZC1 marking separation zone

149

ANSWERS

Chapter 1 – Nautical Terms

1 Steer the boat into the wind.
2 Close hauled, reaching, running.
3 Bow line, stern line, forward backspring, after backspring, forward breast rope, after breast rope.
4 Starboard side.
5 Running before the wind with mainsail and headsail on opposite sides.

Chapter 2 – Ropework

1 For hoisting the sails.
2 Ropes for trimming sails to the correct setting.
3 Multiplait or three strand nylon, 12mm dia. for boats under 7 metres, 16mm for 10 metre craft.
4 For making a loop in a rope which will not slip, typical use for putting over a bollard.
5 Figure of eight knot to prevent sheet slipping through block.

Chapter 3 – Anchorwork

1 Not too close to another vessel or where you will foul their anchor chains, and not in a fairway. Check chart for depth of water at all states of tide and whether bottom is good holding ground.
2 Sand and mud.
3 To mark position of anchor on sea bed.

4 A white light forward where it can best be seen.
5 By marking the chain or rope every few metres or fathoms in a distinctive way (e.g. on chain paint 2 links for 2 metres, 5 links for 5 metres, etc.). On rope do it with binding.

Chapter 4 – Safety

1 Every 3 years or on the expiry date stamped on them.
2 Near the galley and the engine. Easily accessible.
3 Warm clothing, oilskins and seaboots.
4 Compass, barometer, charts, echo sounder, clock.
5 In heavy weather, fog and at night.

Chapter 5 – International Regulations

1 The vessel which has the wind on the port side.
2 The vessel which is to windward.
3 If you have the wind on the port side you keep out of the way of the other vessel.
4 You would be unable to see the other vessel's side lights.
5 Alter course to starboard.
6 The vessel which has the other on her own starboard side.
7 Maintain your course and speed.
8 You may take such action as you may think necessary to avoid collision.
9 Vessel not under command, vessel restricted in her ability to manoeuvre, vessel engaged in fishing, sailing vessel.
10 Vessel not under command, vessel restricted in her ability to manoeuvre, vessel engaged in fishing.
11 Safe speed according to conditions.
12 Stop and navigate with caution.

Chapter 6 – Navigational Terms

1 Nautical miles, equal to approximately 2,000 yards or 1,853 metres or one minute of latitude.

2 One nautical mile per hour.
3 DR takes account of course and distance travelled. EP additionally includes calculations for tidal set and leeway.
4 Either by latitude and longitude, or as a bearing and distance off.
5 A reliable position obtained by cross bearings or similar methods, or by radio bearings or electronic instruments.

Chapter 7 – Navigational Charts and Publications

1 Used to correct charts and bring them up to date.
2 Bottom right hand corner.
3 From the latitude scale.
4 The direction and rate of the tidal stream for every hour before and after high water.
5 To enable the navigator to lay off courses and bearings.

Exercises

1 Course 249° Distance 30.2 miles.
2 Course 055° Distance 17 miles
3 Course 213° Distance 7 miles.

Chapter 9 – Compasses

1 Compass Error 2W.
2 Compass Error 9W.
3 Compass course to steer 164°.
4 True bearing 069°.
5 By comparing the compass readings on different headings with known bearings ashore.

Chapter 10 – Chartwork

1 Course 052° Course to steer to counteract current 060°.
2 Course 069° + 5° for leeway gives a course to steer of 074°.
3 EP at 1200 Lat. 50°47.8′N 0°41.2′E.
4 New course to steer 035.

Chapter 11 – Position Fixing

1 Position at 1230 Lat. 50°50′N Long. 0°37′E.
2 Position Lat. 50°52.1′N Long 0°56.8′E.
3 2 miles off Royal Sovereign Light Vessel.
4 Position at time of second bearing:
  Lat. 50°51.6′N Long 1°31.4°E.
5 Position Lat. 51°08N Long 1°25.4′E.

Chapter 12 – Tides

1 Dover HW 17th June 1201 BST Ht 6.3.
2 Dover LW 18th August 0849 BST Ht 0.9.
                    2109 BST Ht 0.8.
3 Hastings HW 0106 7.2 1330 7.4 BST
  Hastings LW 0819 0.9 2039 0.8 BST.
4 Richborough HW 0134 5.6 1358 5.6 BST
            LW 0906 0.8 2122 0.7 BST.

Chapter 13 – Pilotage

1 A bearing of two navigational objects in line.
2 Single bearings of navigational objects which will keep you clear of danger.
3 Watch for other vessels, keep to starboard side of channel, allow for wind and tide, keep a look out for overtaking craft, pass buoys with plenty of room, remember deep water is on outside of bends.
4 Starboard. It is a port hand buoy coming in.
5 Pass to the north. It is a cardinal buoy marking the northern limit of a danger.

Chapter 14 – Visual aids to navigation

1 Characteristic of light, range, colour, height of tower. Also fog signals and radio beacons, if any.
2 Group flashing, 3 flashes every 15 seconds, height of lighthouse 40 metres, range of visibility 27 miles. Additional fixed red and green lights at 37 metres height.

3 A light which goes out periodically as opposed to flashing on periodically.

4 In metres above MHWS.

5 Because they may be activated by light and could be in clear weather when there is fog a short distance down the coast. Also because direction sound is coming from can be deceptive in fog.

Chapter 15 – Passage Planning

1 Changes of course, wind direction and force, distance covered by log reading, times of sighting or passing buoys, lighthouses, headlands, etc with bearings, times of switching engine on or off.

2 Nautical almanacs, charts, pilot books with diagrams of harbours.

3 By notifying them of your intended passage, intended destination and details of craft so they have vital information if notified by shore contact you are overdue.

4 Expected Time of Arrival.

Chapter 16 – Restricted Visibility

1 So your craft can be seen on radar screen of other vessels.

2 By using a radio direction set, or electronic navigation instrument, or by following a line of soundings on the chart. If not possible keep careful DR plot.

3 A prolonged blast followed by two short blasts every minute, but a small vessel may make any efficient sound signal.

4 Power driven vessel under way.

5 Fix and plot position, check radar reflector in place, ensure good visual and listening look-out, prepare to make sound signals, get crew into lifejackets.

Chapter 17 – Meteorology

1 An indication of wind force.

2 0033hrs, 0555hrs, 1355hrs, 1750hrs.

3 Land heating up during the day, causing wind to blow in from the sea.

4 Wind, rain, moderate visibility. Possibility of gales.
5 When wind is expected to reach force 8 or more.

Additional Exercises

1 Compass course 173° Distance 7.4 miles.
2 Compass course allowing for current and leeway 198°.
3 Position 50°46.1'N 0°24.2'E.
4 Position at 1200 50°48.5'N 0°34.1'E.
5 First course 227° Distance 16 miles. Second course 184° distance 7.6 miles. ETA 1315.
6 Height of tide at Portsmouth on 1st June 2.5 metres at 1200 BST.
7 Distance off Beachy Head Lt House is 3 miles.
9 Position of Varne Lt Vessel 51°01.1N 1°24'E
  Buoy ZCI   50°45N 1°27'E

INDEX

OTHER BOOKS FOR YACHTSMEN FROM DAVID & CHARLES

The Concise Yachtmaster Guide
by Mike Bowyer
A follow on to The Concise Day Skipper Guide

Astro Navigation by Calculator
by Henry Levison

Exercises in Pilotage
by John Anderson

The Sailing Cruiser Manual
by John Mellor

Ocean Cruising Countdown
by Geoff Pack

One Watch At A Time
by Kim Nouak
Around the world with *Drum* on the Whitbread Race

The Shell Book of Seamanship
by John Russell

Shipshape: The Art of Sailboat Maintenance
by Ferenc Maté

Start With A Hull: Fitting Out A GRP Hull From Start To Finish
by Loris Goring

The Story of Yachting
by Ranulf Ragner & Tim Thompson

Topsail and Battleaxe
by Tom Cunliffe
A voyage in the wake of the Vikings

Wind And Sailing Boats
by Alan Watts

Yachtmaster Offshore: The Art of Seamanship
by John Russell